AF604516

WE GO TOGETHER

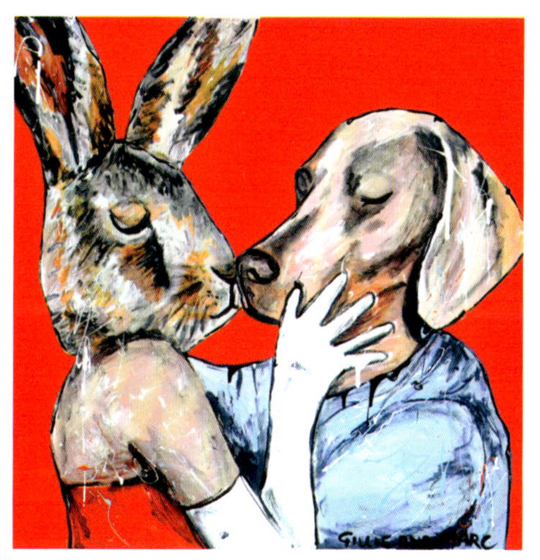

GILLIE AND MARC

Gillie and Marc Schattner
Unit 16, 77 Bourke Road, Alexandria
Sydney, NSW 2015, Australia
Telephone: +61 2 9700 7103
www.gillieandmarc.com

ISBN 9780646946535

Front cover
*He loved the way she held him
tight when they went really fast*
Mixed media on card
80 x 60cm
2015

Title page
She thought, kiss me like it's our first kiss
Acrylic on board
91 x 91cm
2015

Book design by Gillie Schattner
Printed by Shenzhen Candidus Printing Group

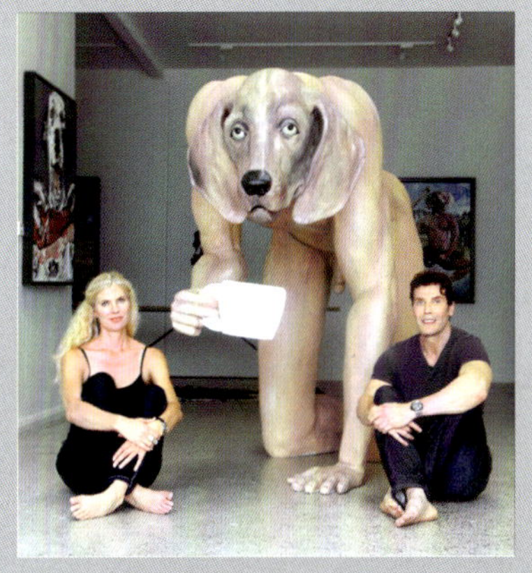

Australian artists Gillie and Marc first introduced 'Dogman' in 2009 with their infamous sculpture Good Boy, which made headlines around the world because it combined the ancient mythology of cynocephaly – the placement of a dog's head on a human body – with full-frontal nudity.

An expression of the canine qualities Gillie and Marc admire and wish to see more of in mankind, the Dogman hybrid represents honesty, non-judgement, unselfishness, and altruism.

When Dogman met his mate 'Rabbitgirl' in 2010, he found another free-spirited, good-natured creature that didn't shy away from emotional availability. Rabbitgirl, like Dogman, was ready to take on the world with somebody.

The pair have been together – living, loving, travelling and learning – ever since. They are wildly different on the outside, but on the inside they are one.

We are all different, and that's
what makes togetherness
so important

GILLIE AND MARC

Life with you means taking turns on the back seat

He loved exercising his legs because he was worried he had small calves
Acrylic on board
91 x 91cm
2015

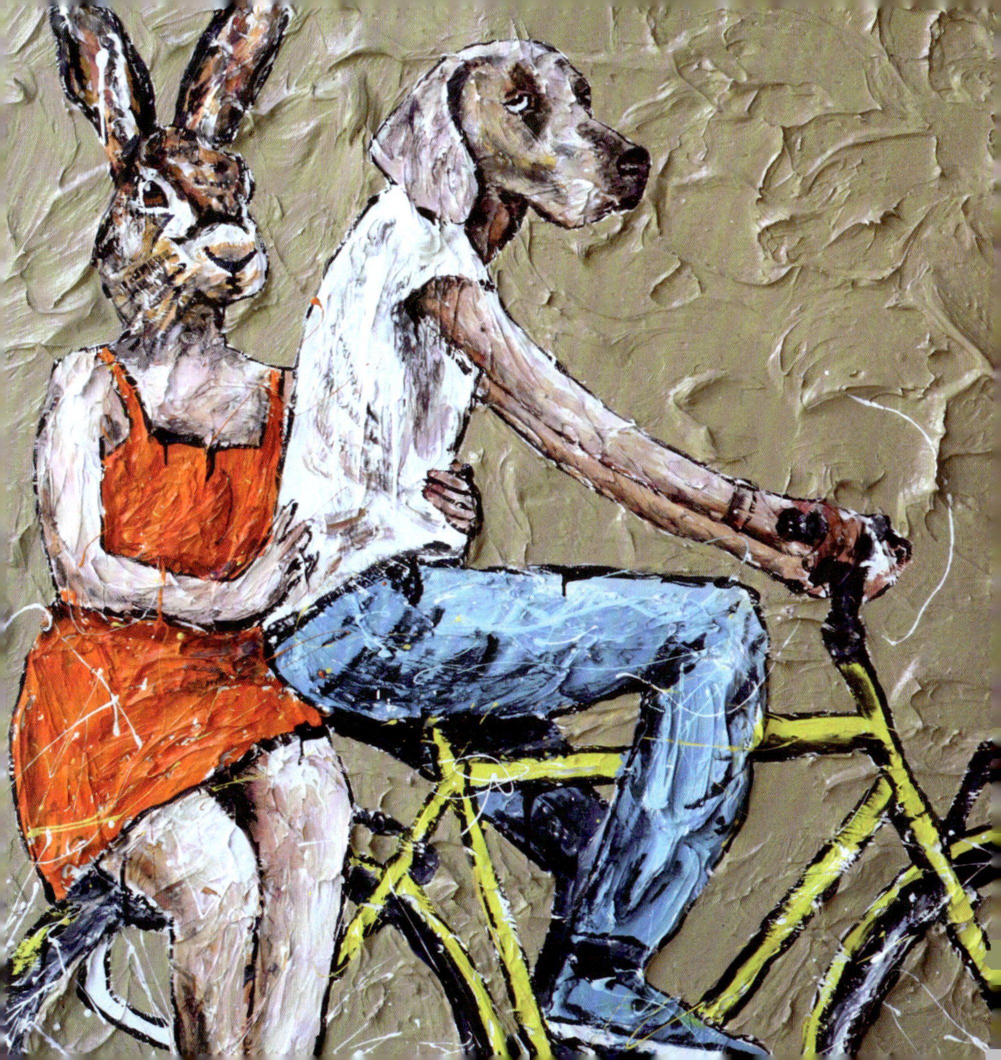

I couldn't make it without my co-pilot

Rabbitgirl and Dogman in Aston Martin
Polyresin
19 x 32 x 14cm
2015

Photography by James Moffatt

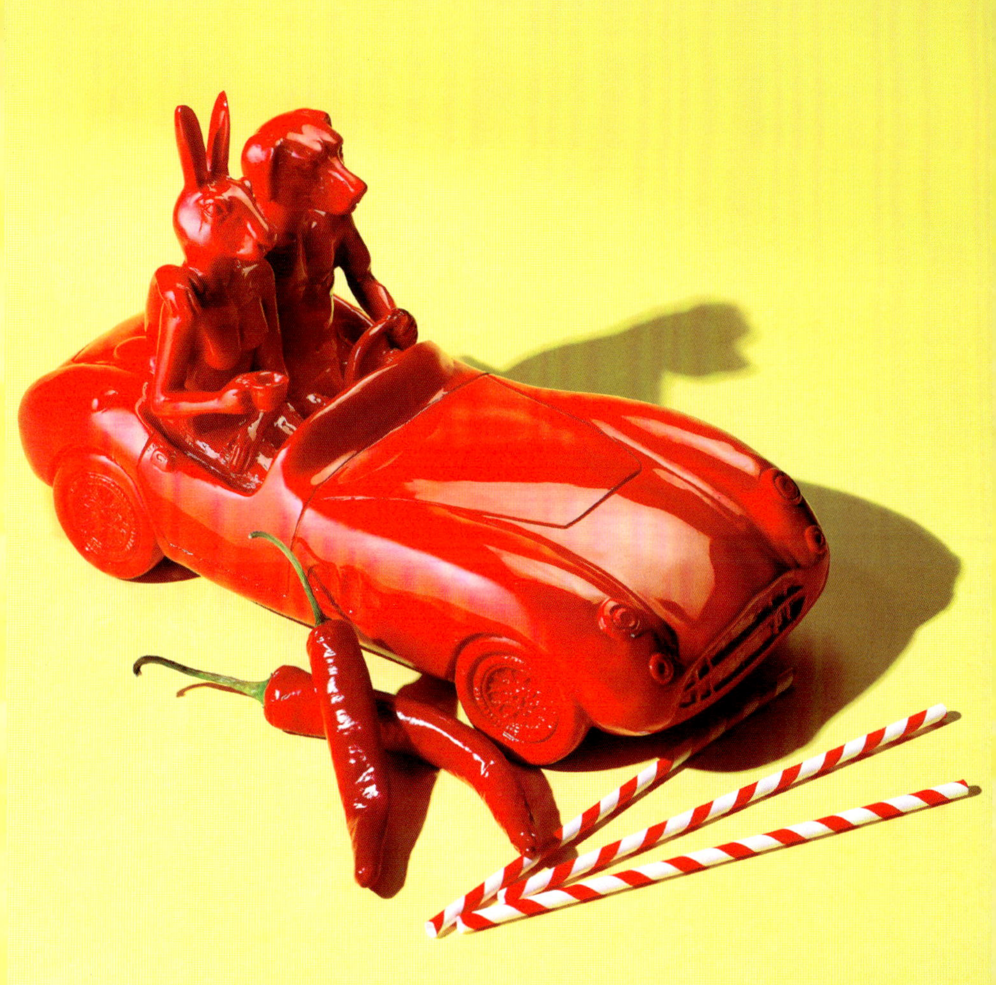

It takes two to argue, but only one to end it

It takes two
Permanently installed in Paddington, Sydney
Bronze
180 x 160cm
2012

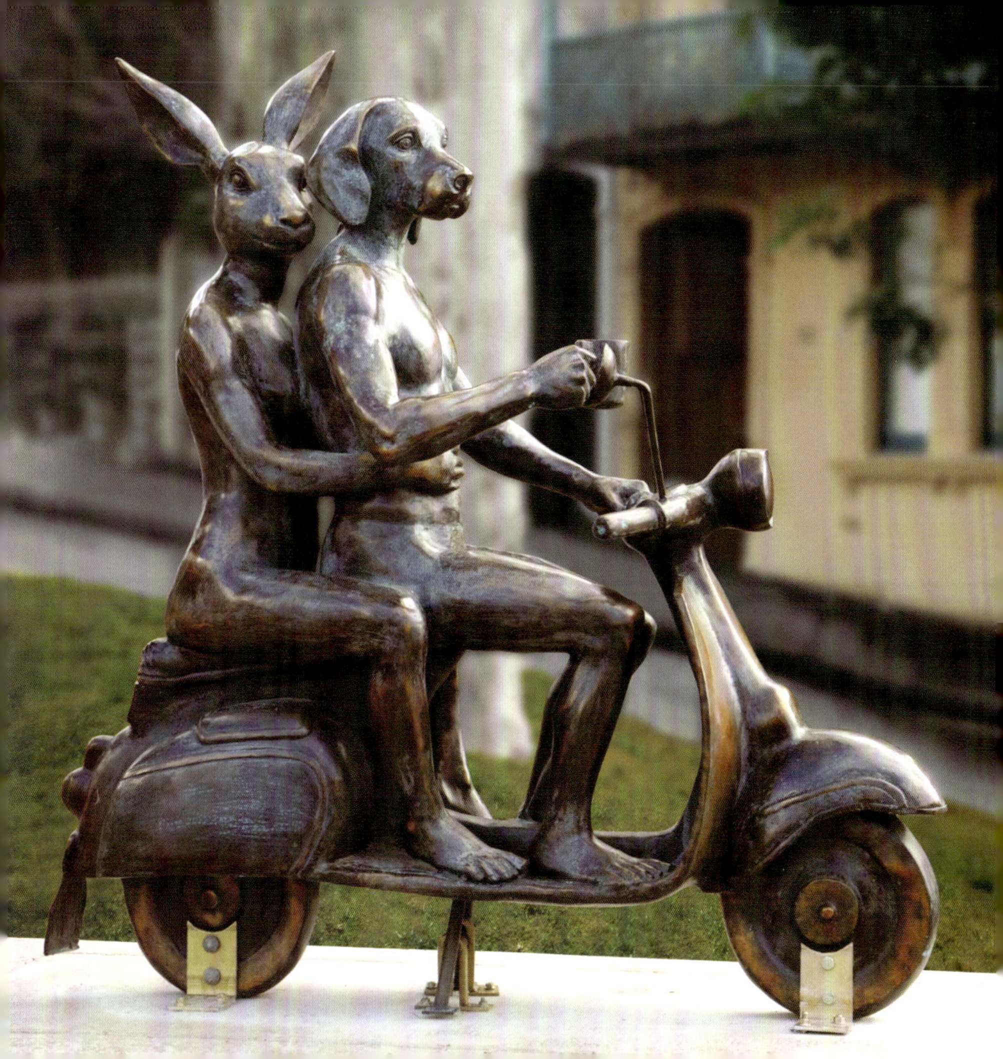

If we can make it here, we'll make it anywhere

Statue of Liberty NYC with love
Dogman and Rabbitgirl
Mixed media on card
80 x 60cm
2015

NEW YORK
GILLIE AND MARC

There's always a place to wash worries away

Bathtime
Photographic print
85 x 127cm
2014

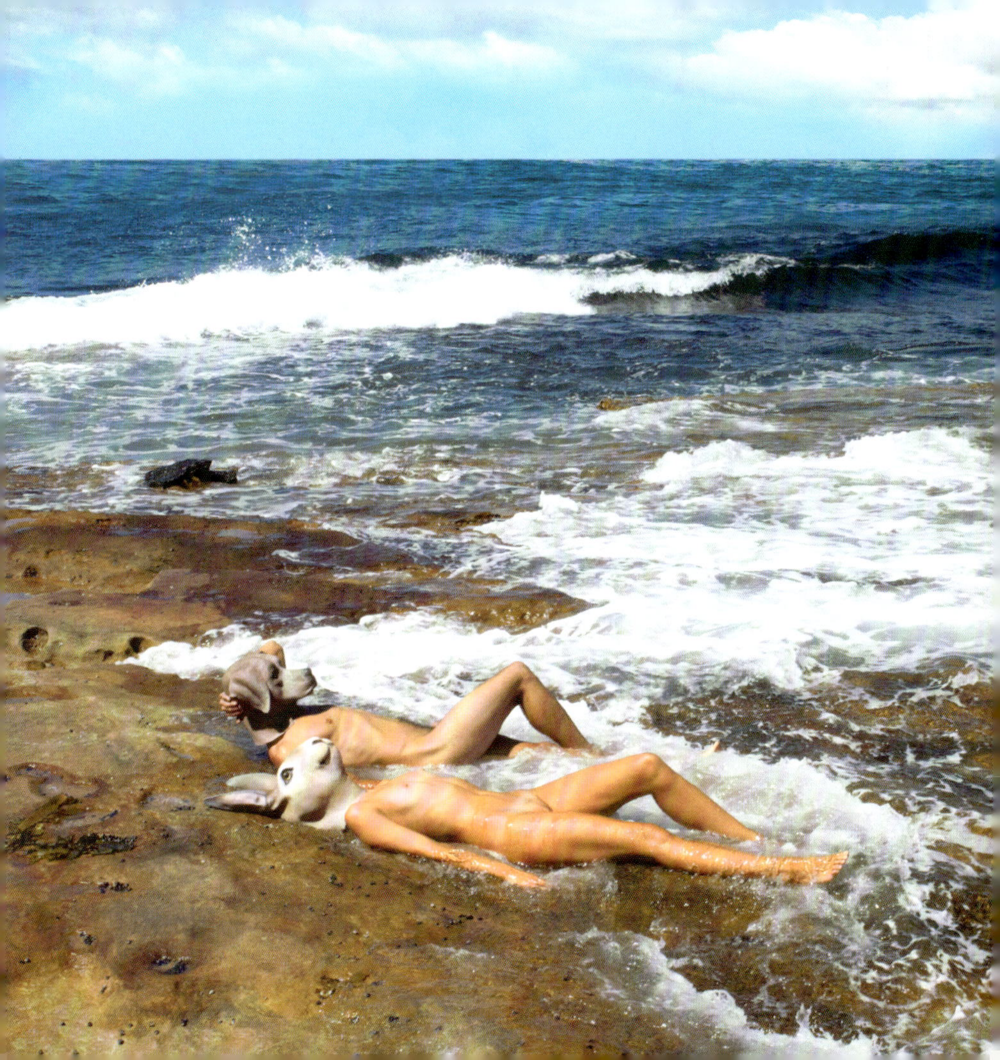

Love is a balance of holding on and letting go

He thought some days you ride alone but it was so much better to ride together
Acrylic on canvas
100 x 100cm
2014

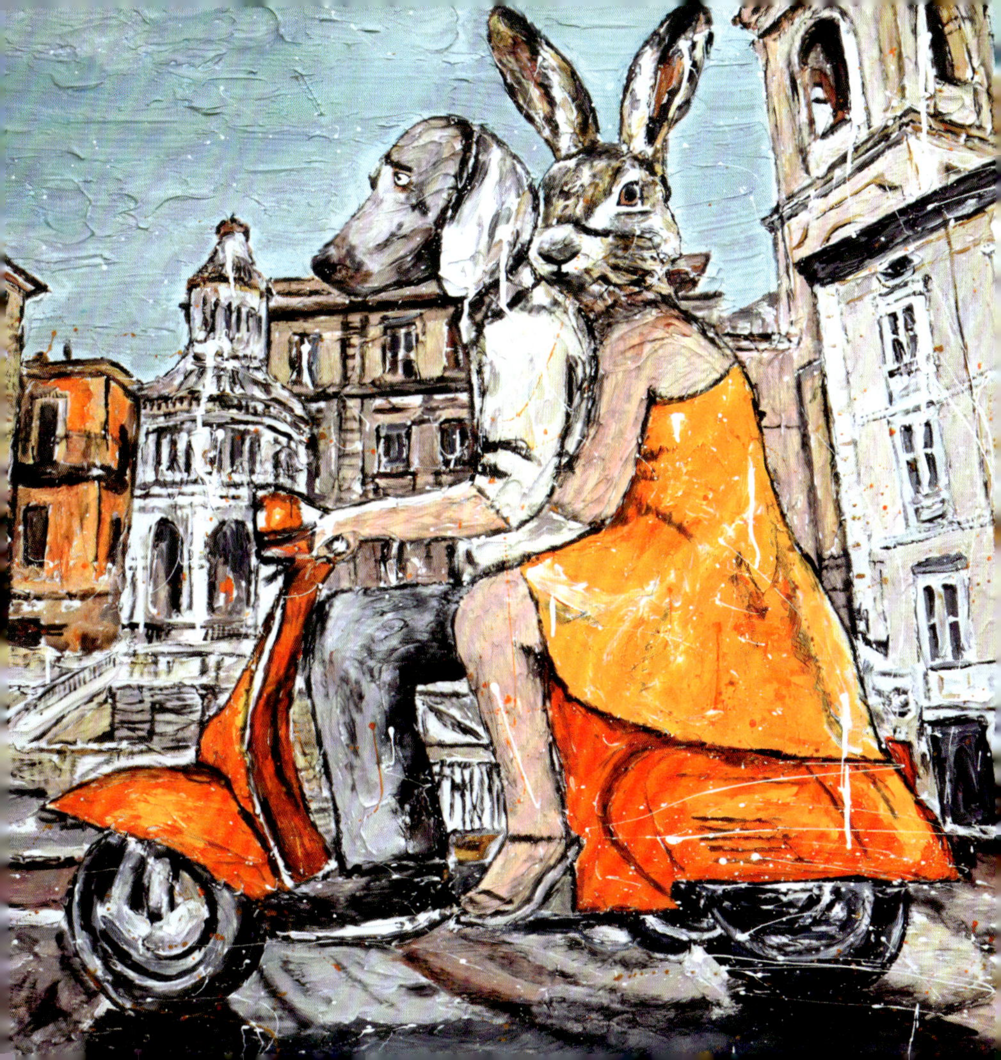

Just because I took off the roof, doesn't mean we're going to get wet

They loved driving their Beetle Convertible around the sunny shores of the South of France
Fibreglass and 2pak paint
36 x 50 x 24cm
2015

Photography by James Moffatt

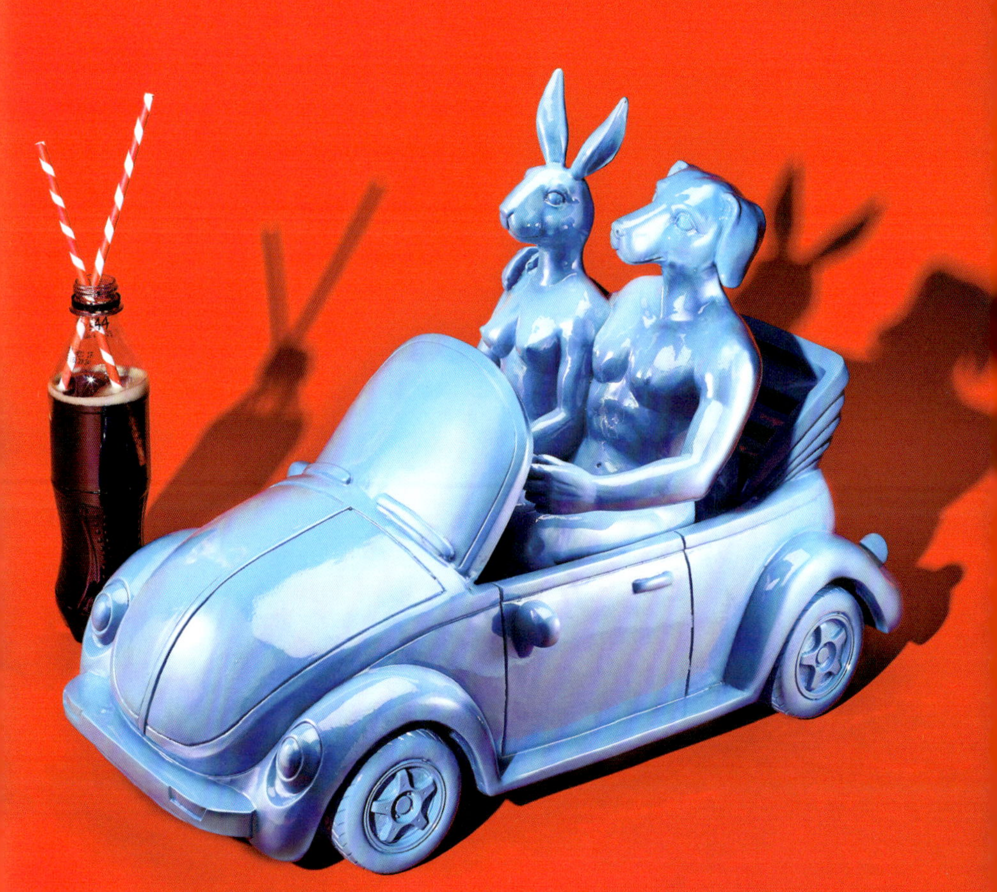

Everything is always better with coffee

Coffee Drinkers
Permanently installed in Rundle Mall, Adelaide
Bronze
168 x 200 x 90cm
2013

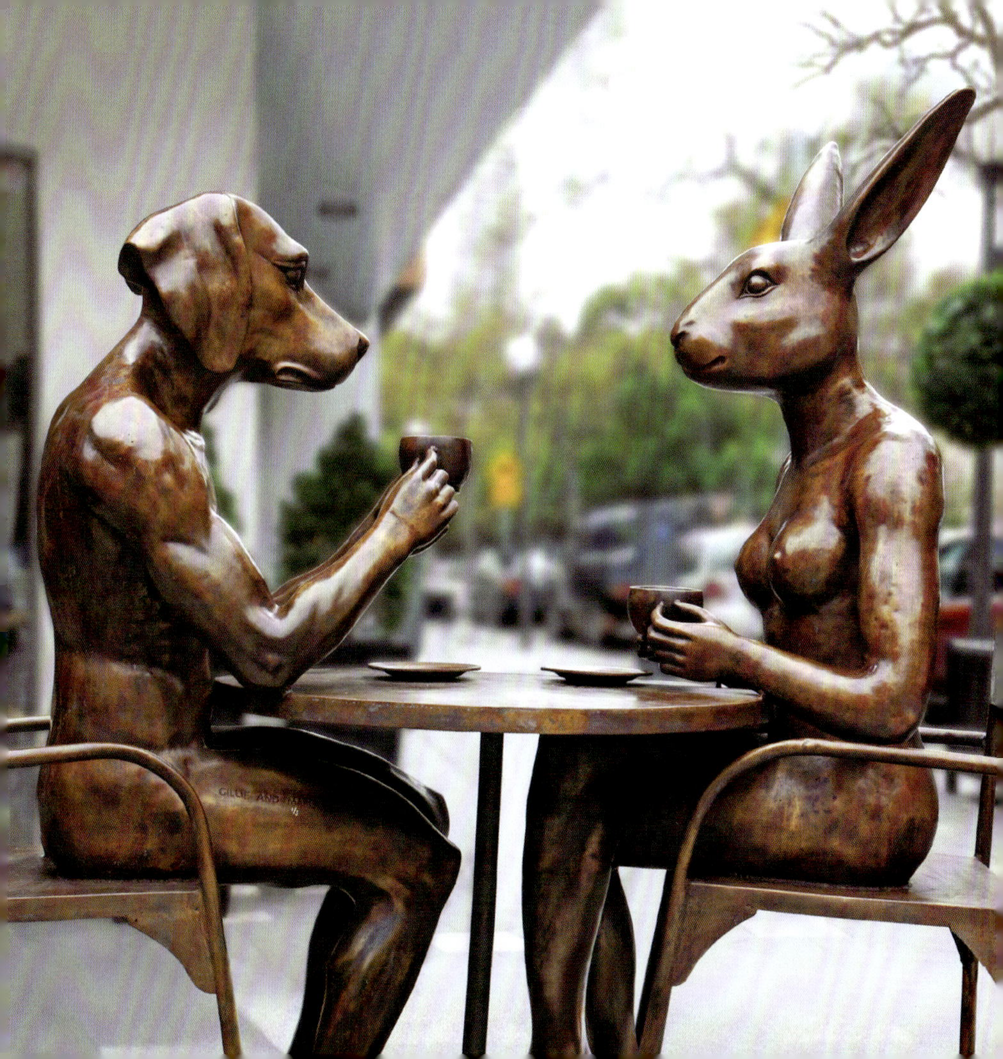

Popsicles are sweeter in the company of another

They both wanted the yellow
popsicle but he let her have it
Bondi Beach, Sydney
Acrylic on wall
200 x 400cm
2015

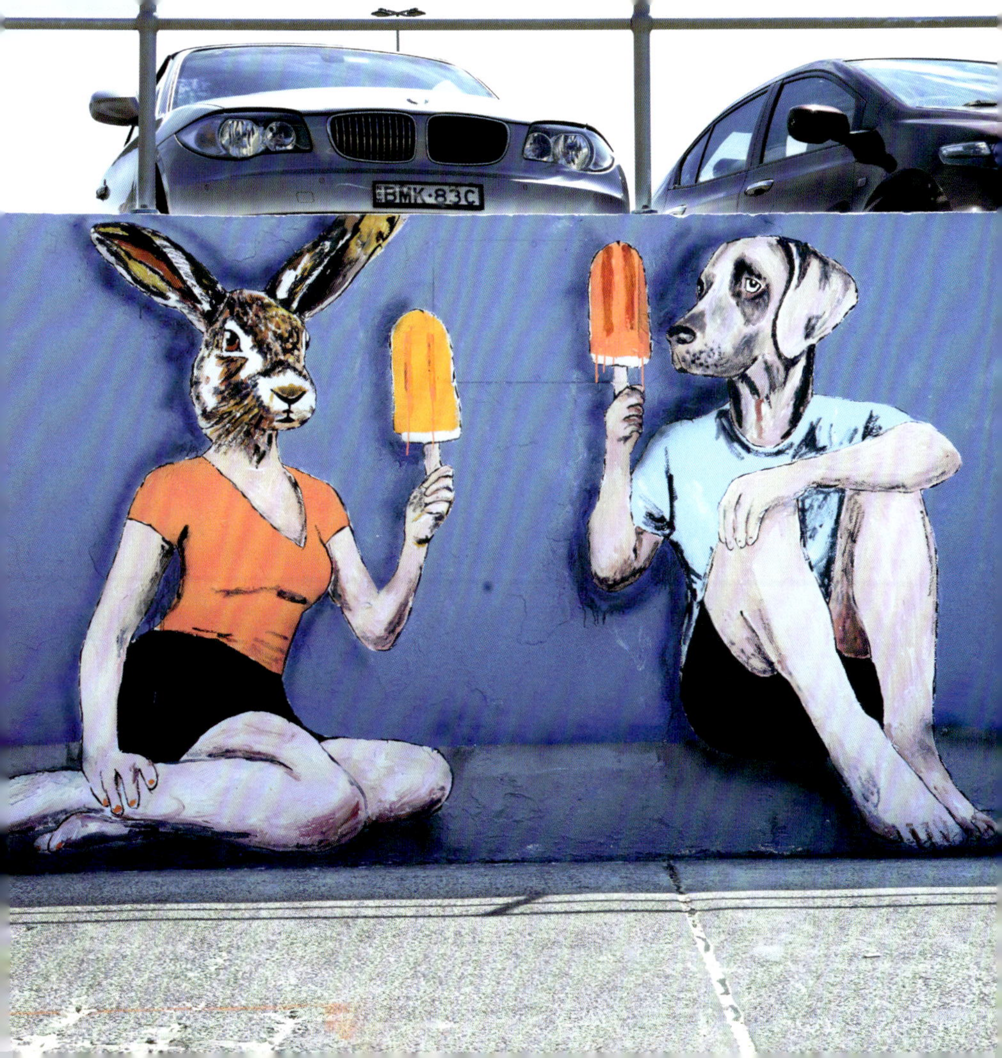
BMK·83C

If we understand each other's silence, we will understand each other's words

She understood every word he said even though they spoke a different language
Photographic print
85 x 127cm
2014

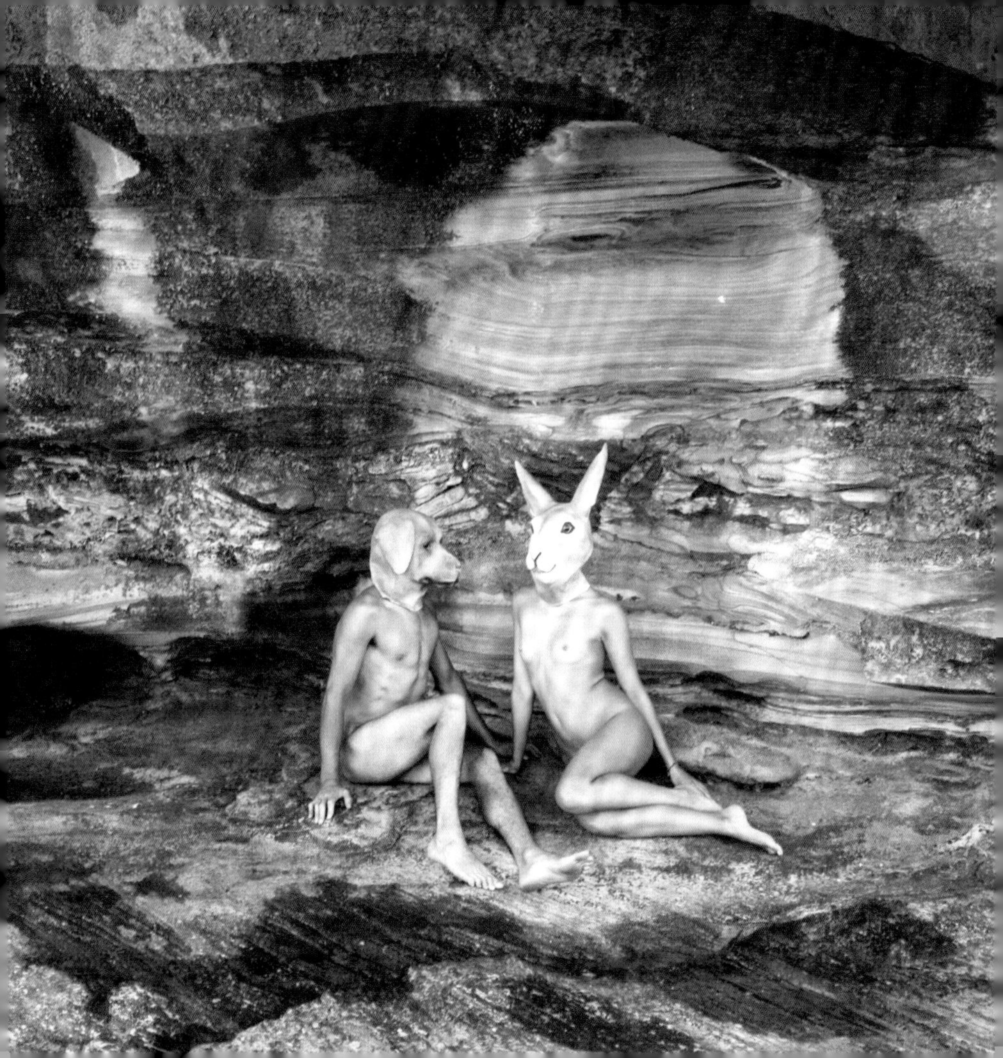

The best testimony of love is trust

Living the high life with their new friend allowed them to see places they never imagined, even if it did mean sore bottoms
Acrylic on canvas
120 x 120cm
2011

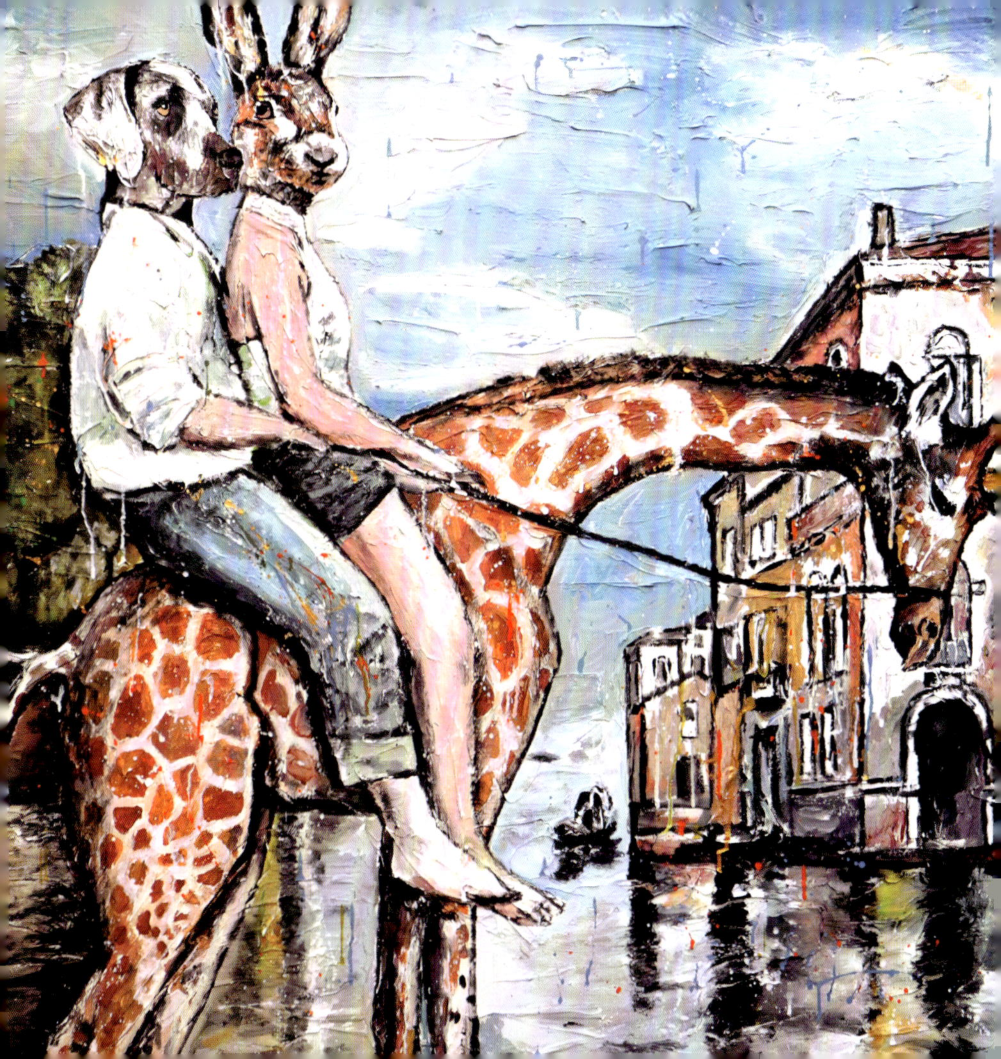

Everyone needs to escape sometimes

Vespa Riders
Polyresin
48 x 50 x 18cm
2014

Photography by James Moffatt

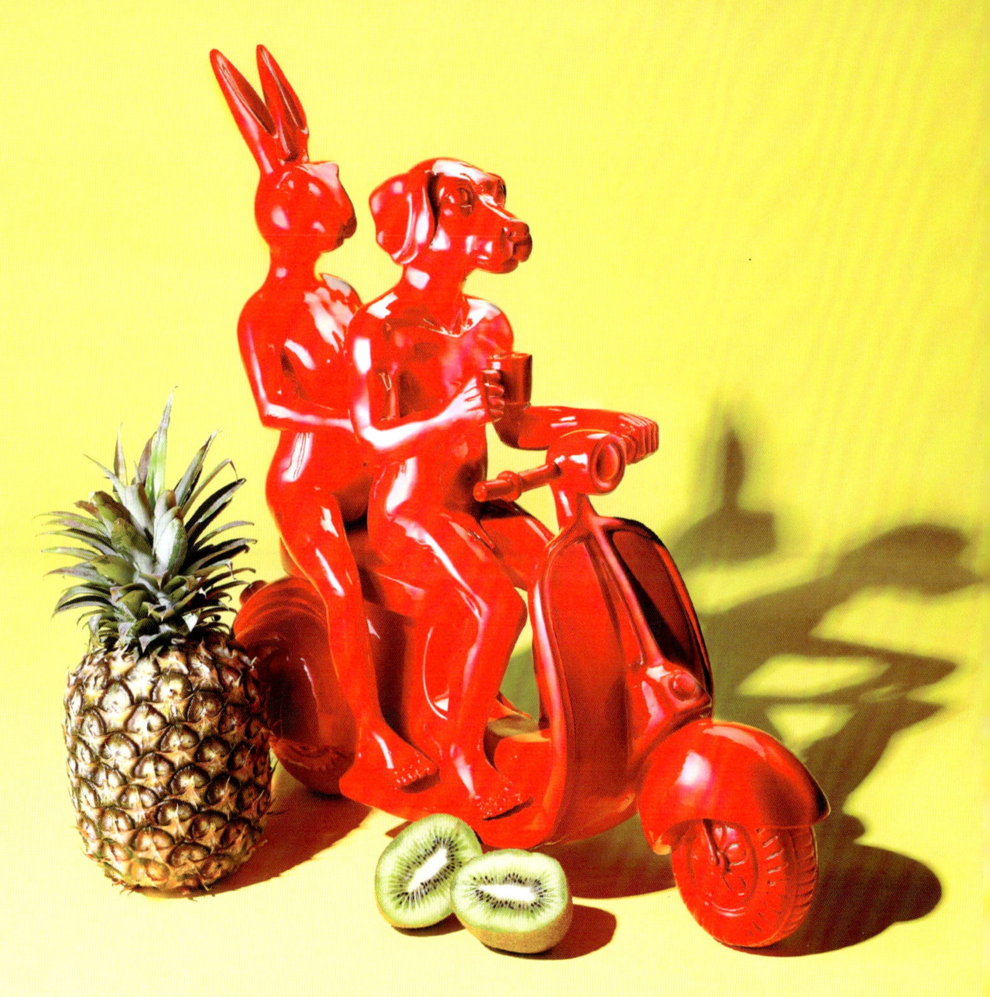

The best view comes after the hardest climb

The travellers have arrived
Featured in 2012 Sculptures by the Sea, Bondi
Now installed permanently at McClelland Gallery & Sculpture Park, Victoria
Fibreglass and bronze paint
236 x 180 x 85cm
2012

Photography by Gary P. Hayes

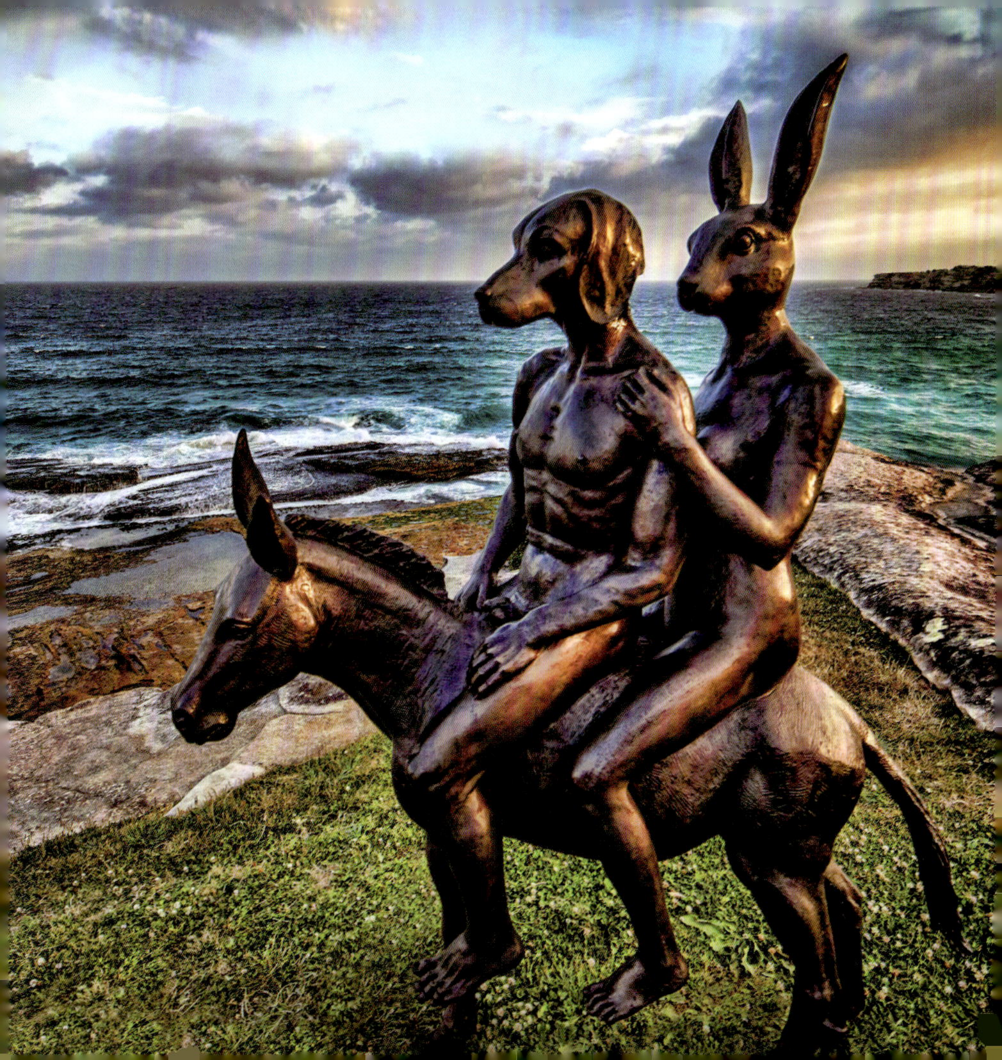

Life is better with wind in your hair

He loved the way she held him tight when they went really fast
Mixed media on card
80 x 60cm
2015

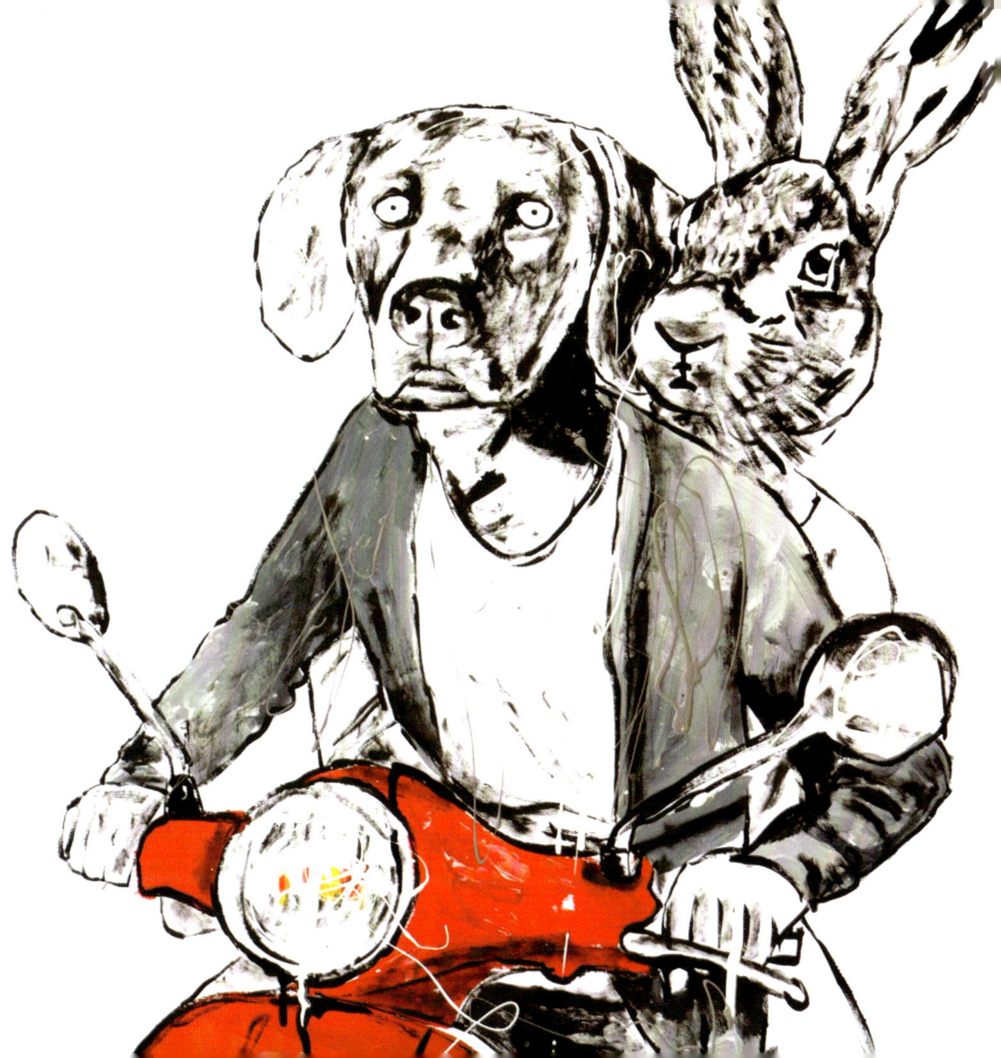

The naked truth is more important than the best-dressed lie

Her ears were much longer than his but he loved how he could hear the sound of the sea in them
Photographic print
85 x 127cm
2014

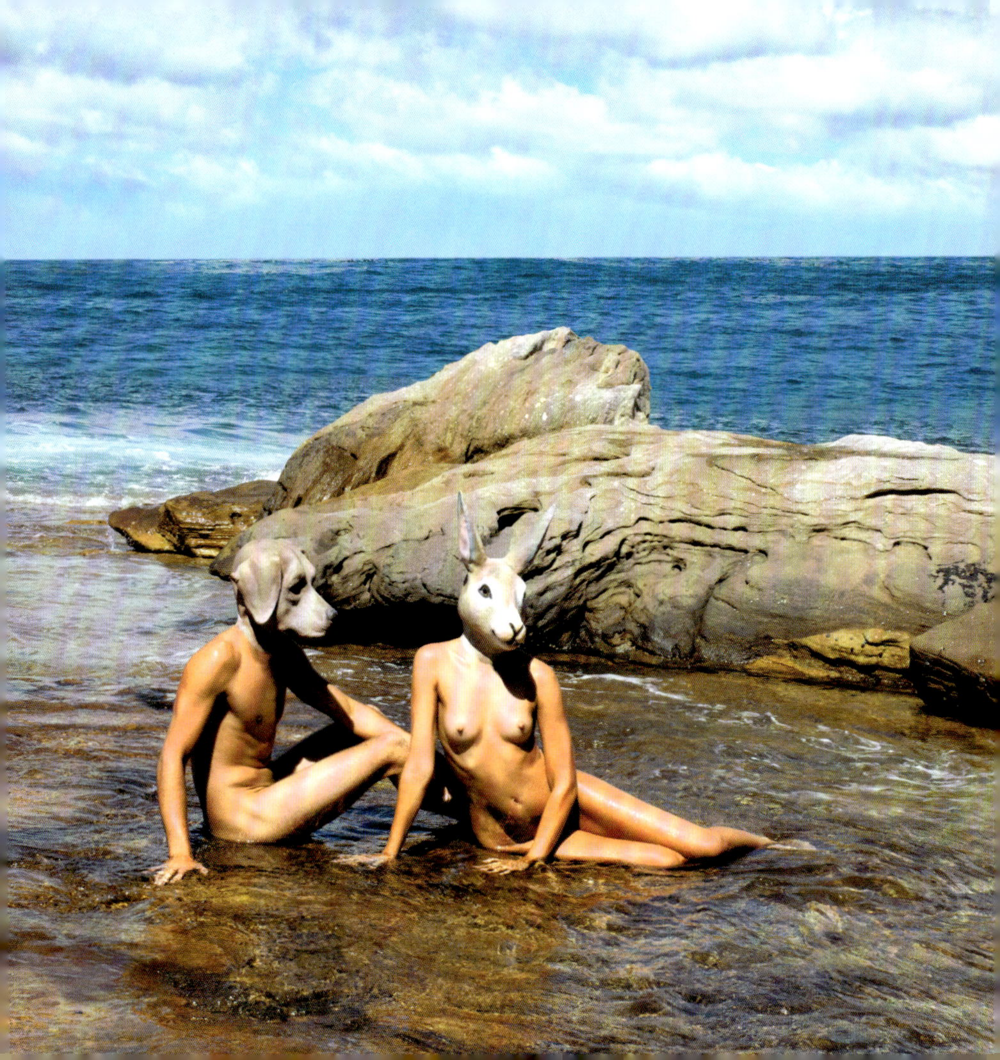

The only person I want to share the world with today is you

She never wanted to forget this moment, and iPhone 5 was the answer
Acrylic on board
91 x 91cm
2014

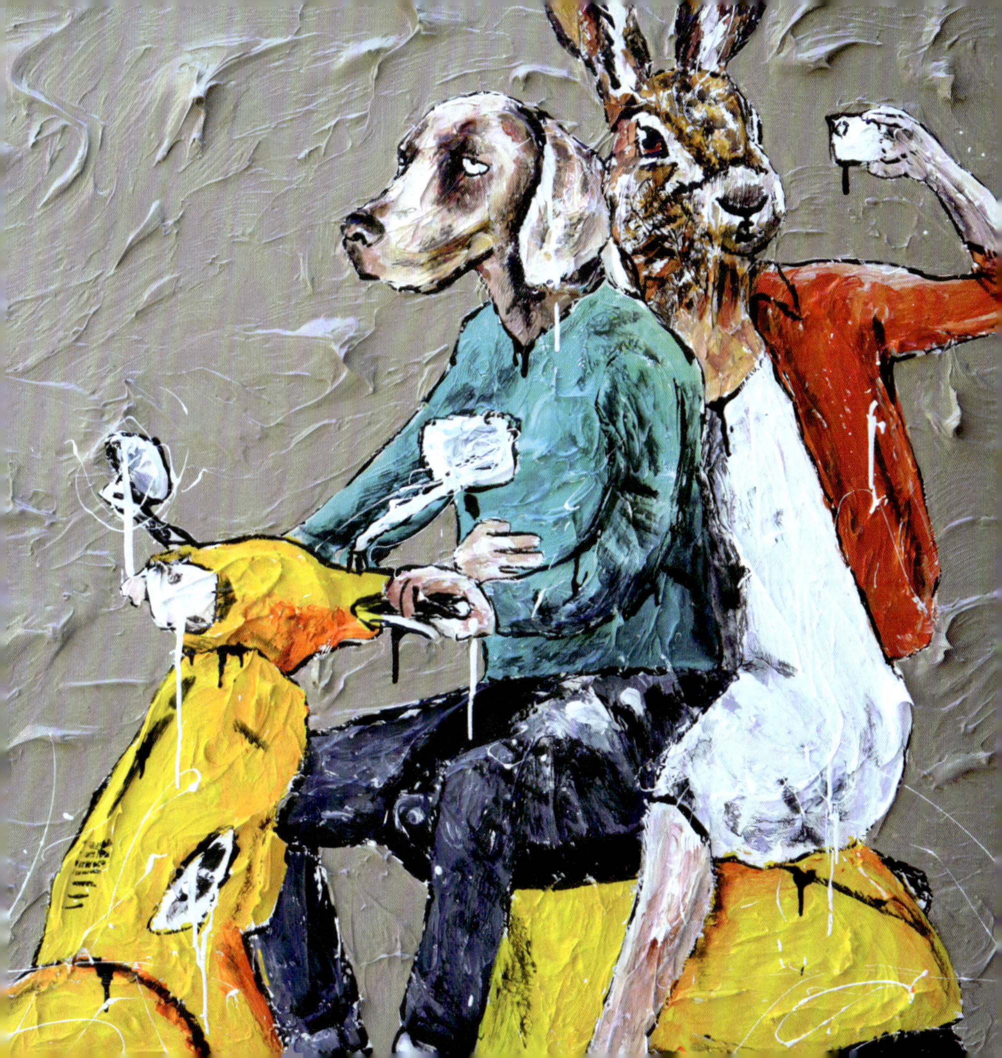

Contemplation is the most rewarding activity

Right: *Mini lolly Rabbitgirl*
Left: *Mini lolly Dogman*
Clear Polyresin
26.5 and18.5cm high
2015

Photography by James Moffatt

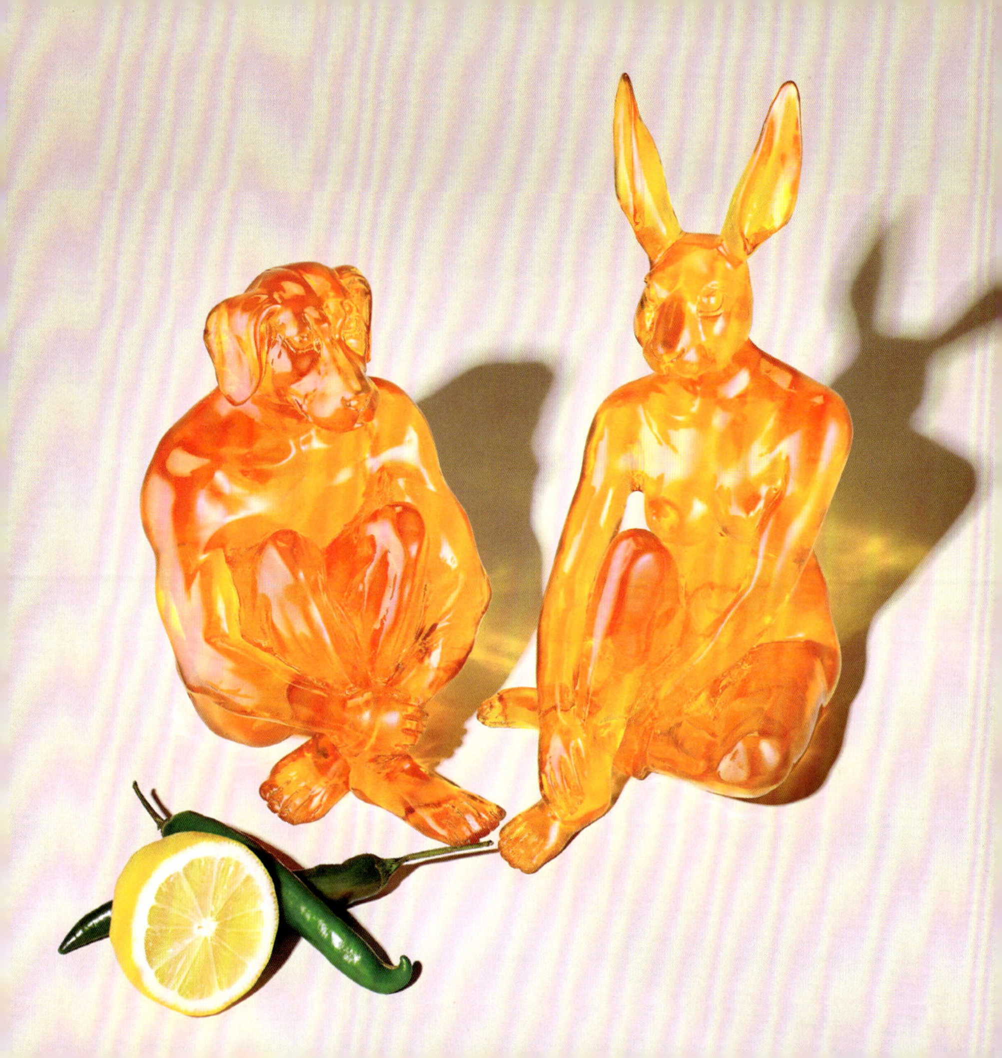

Adventures will always be better together

Tandem Riders
Permanently installed in Beaufort Street, Perth
Bronze
220 x 275 x 70cm
2013

Photography by Jeremy Atlan of 3P Photography

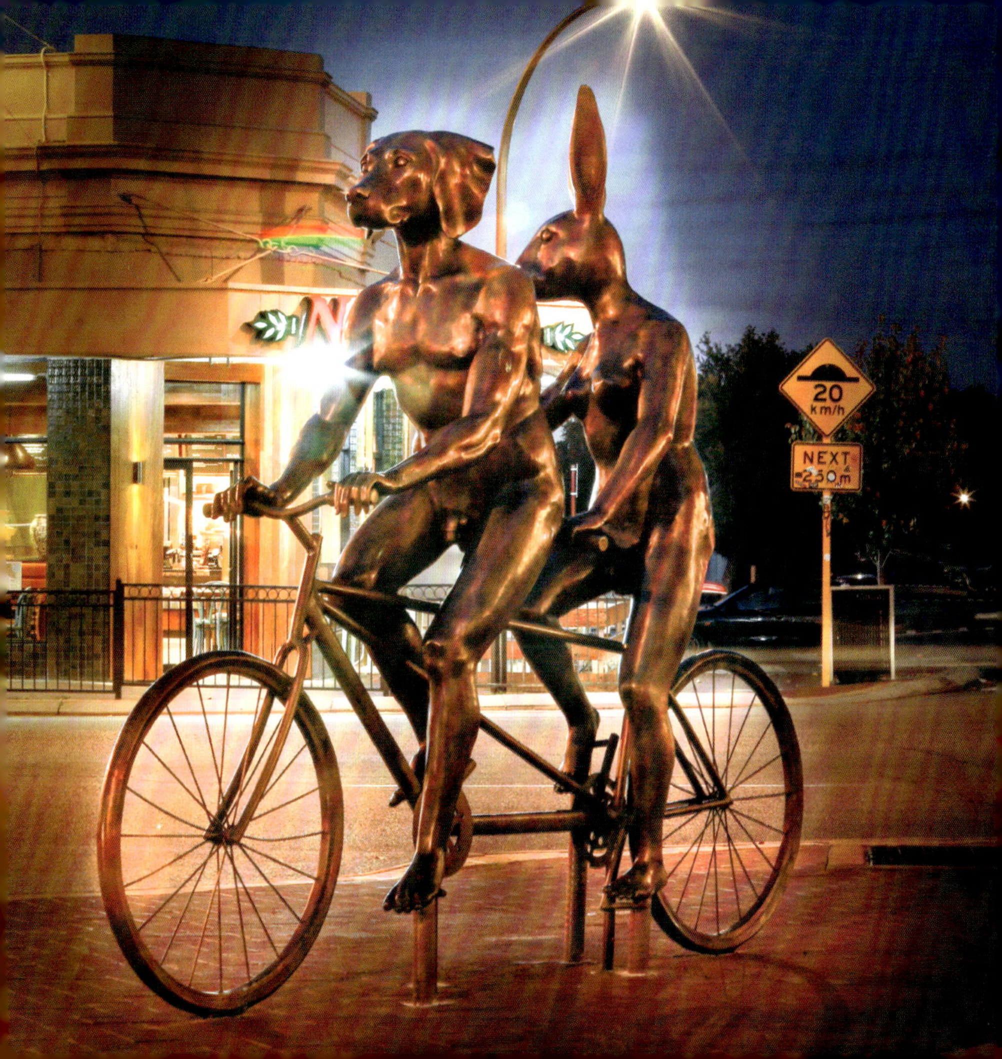
20
km/h
NEXT

Travel not to escape life, but so life doesn't escape us

She hoped for an unexpected surprise and this was it
Mixed media on card
80 x 60cm
2015

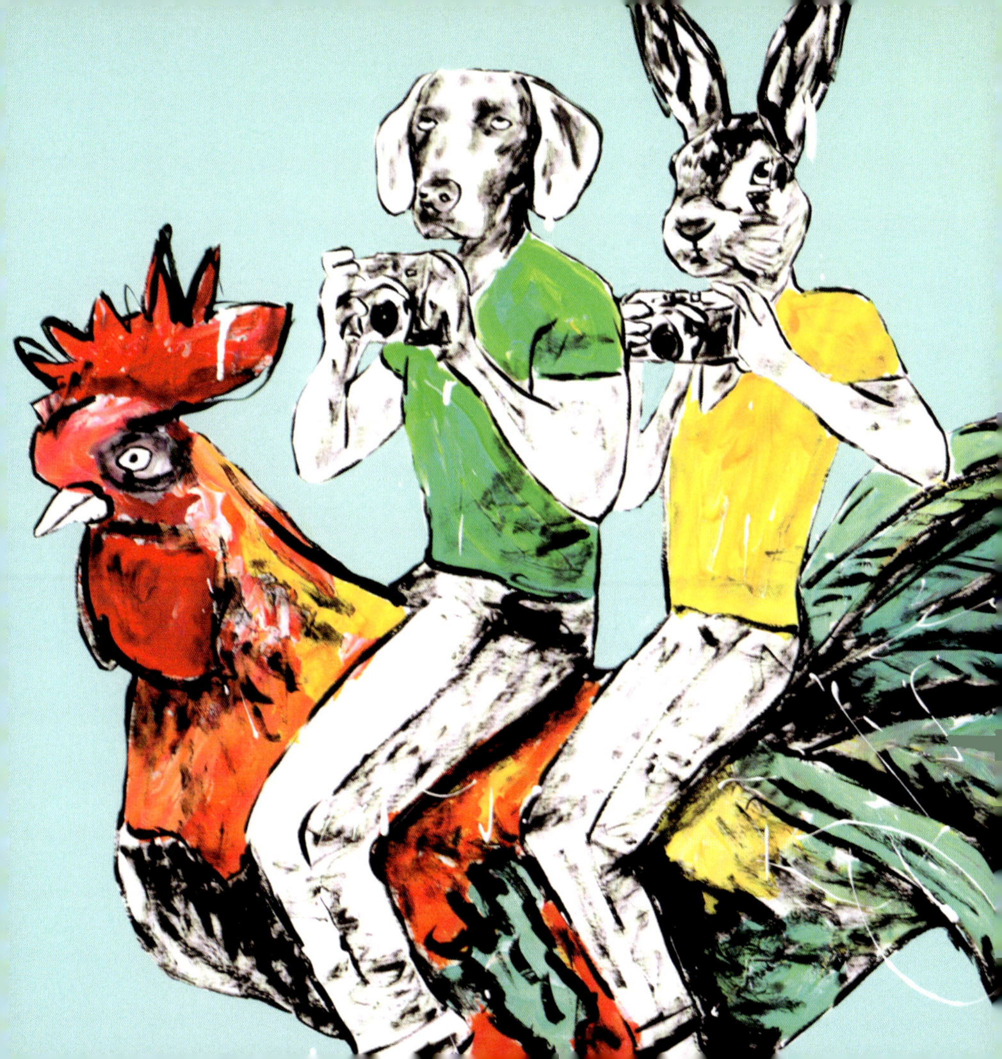

We're not like everybody else. That's a good thing

He loved his Maserati but this was even more exotic
Acrylic on board
91 x 91cm
2014

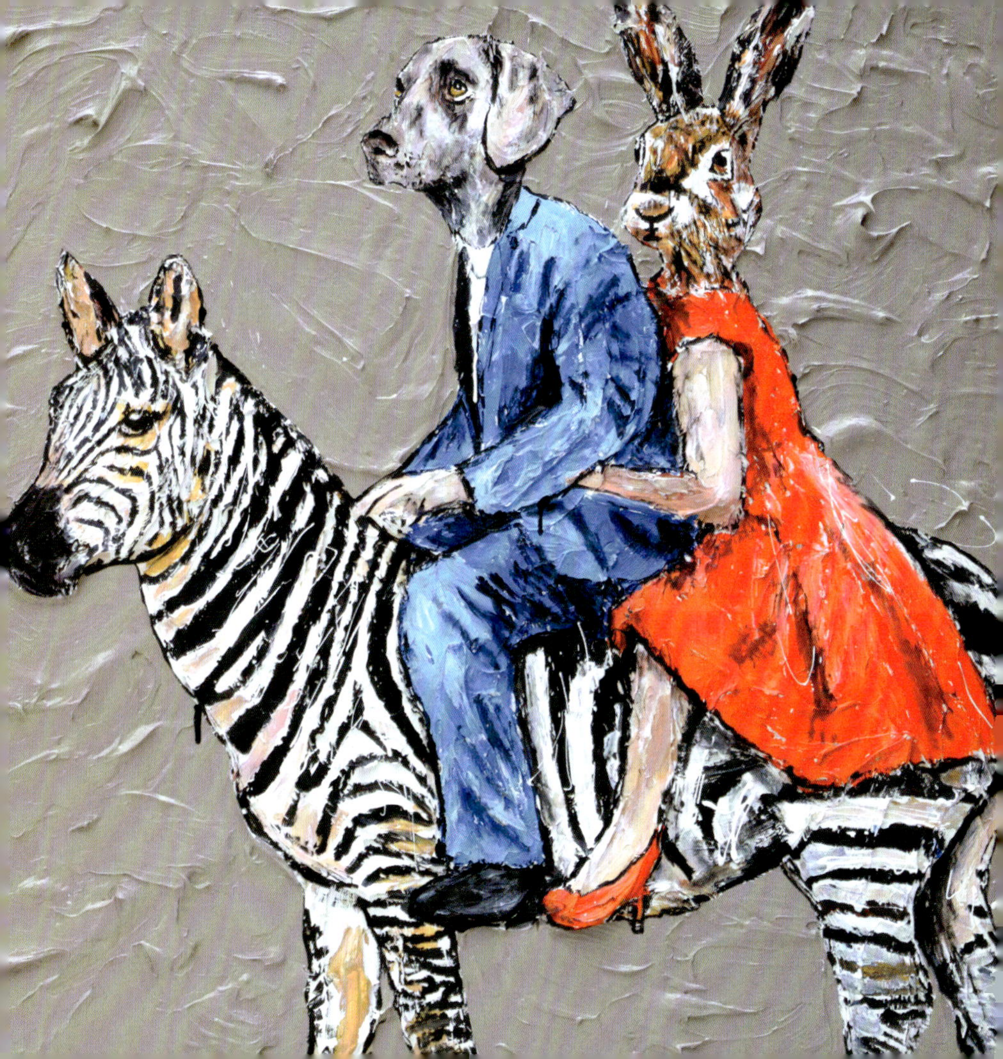

Don’t let the seeds stop you from enjoying the melon

Right: *Lost Dog*
Left: *Lost Rabbit*
Fibreglass and 2pak paint
67cm and 89cm high
2014

Photography by James Moffatt

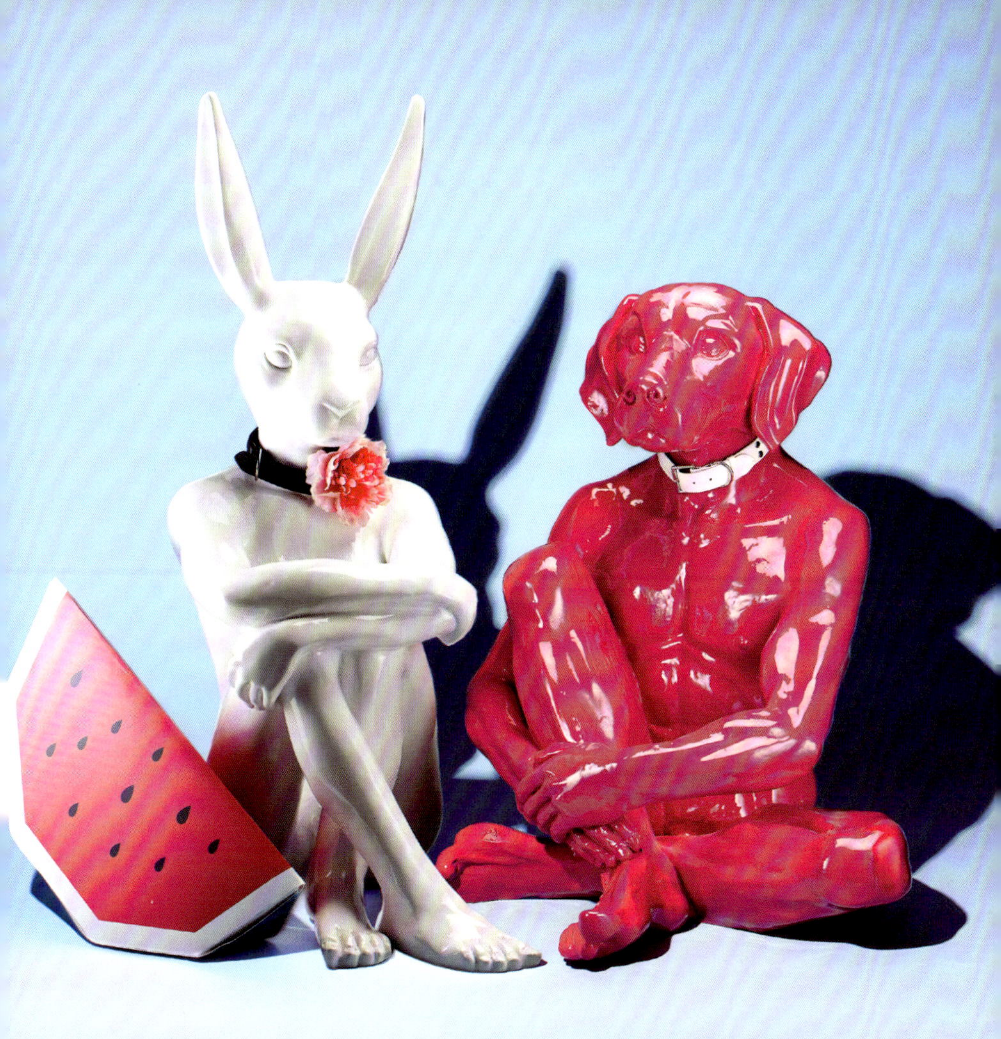

Surfing is like making love.
No matter how many times
you've done it, it feels good

The Wave Riders
Exhibited in The Harbour Sculpture Prize 2015, Woolwich
and later at Woolloomooloo Wharf, Sydney
Bronze
250 x 290 x 170cm
2015

Photography by Jessie Schattner

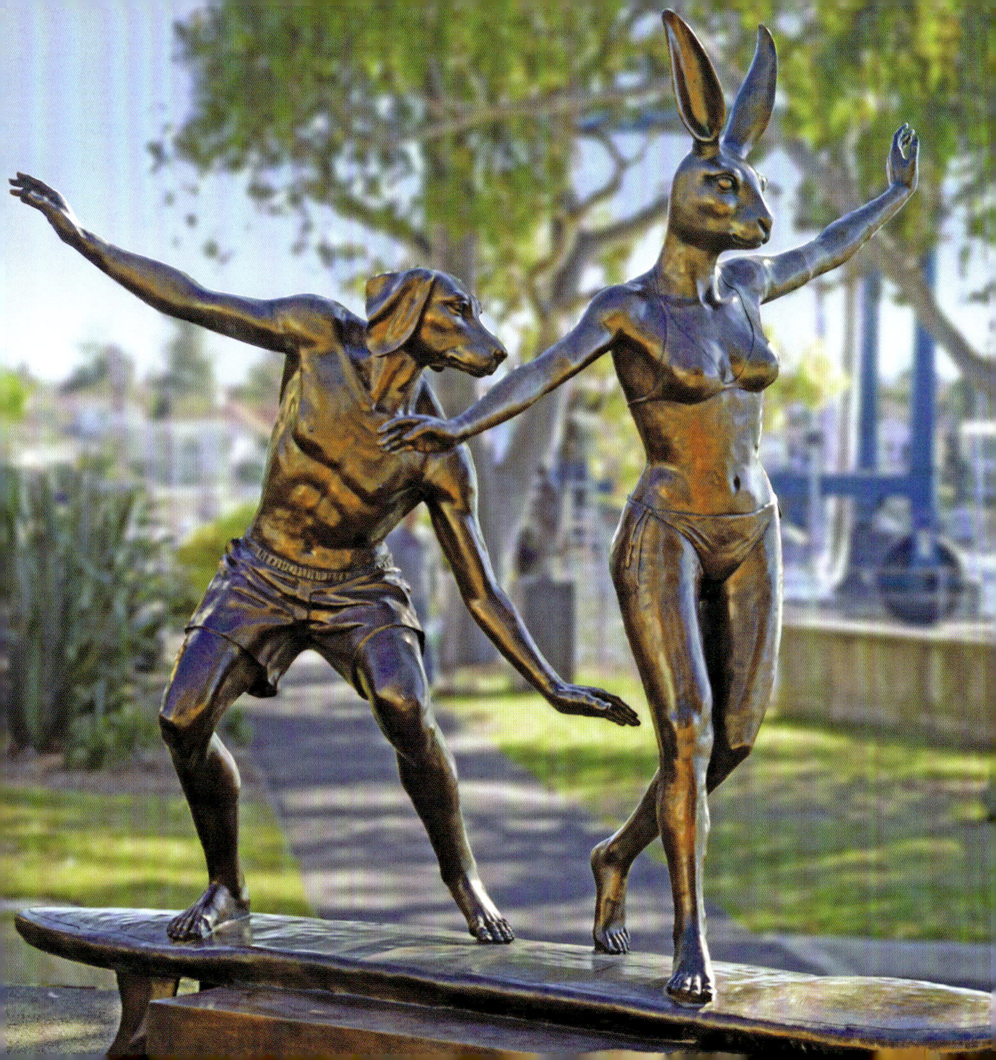

When we hold hands, we're telling the world that we're proud of each other

He sang to her, 'I want to hold your hand' and she did
Mixed media on card
80 x 60cm
2015

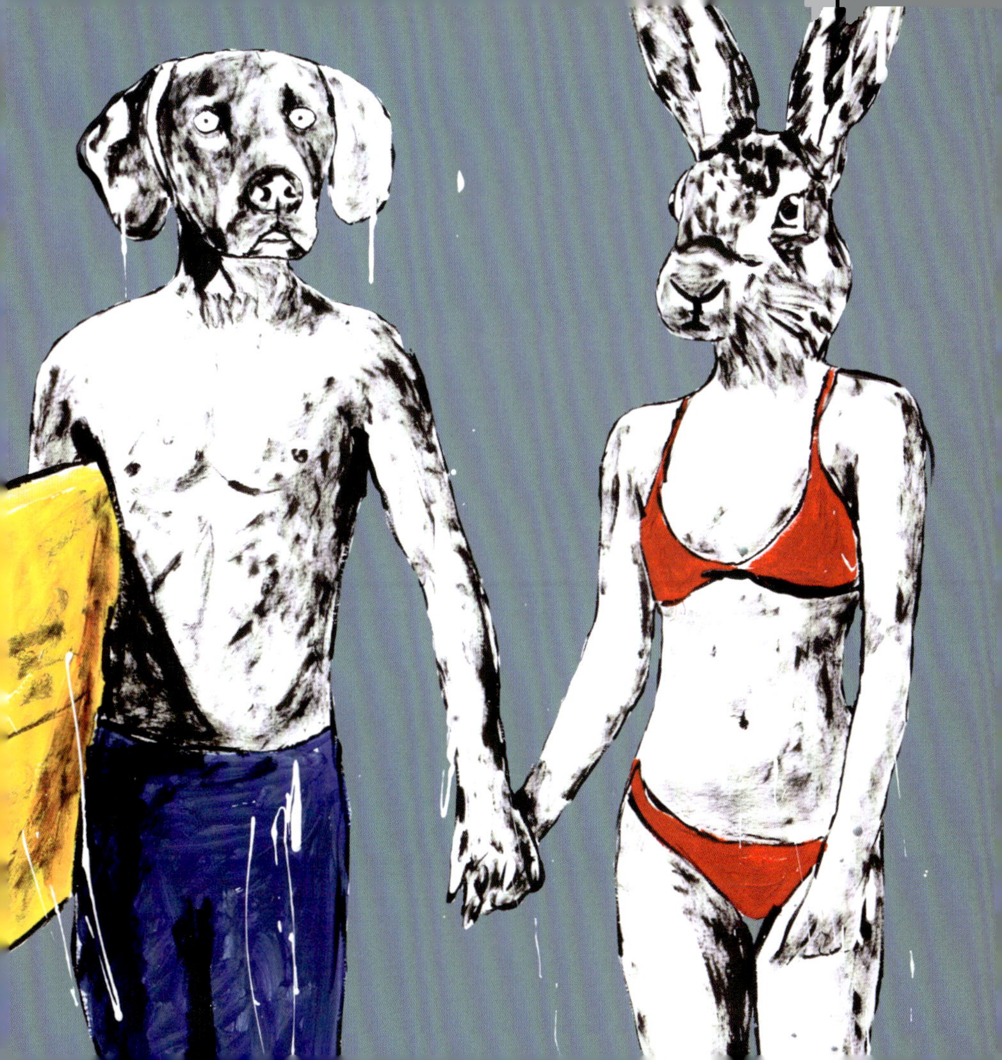

Life is like jazz.
It's best when improvised

They loved in the photobooth
Acrylic on canvas
76 x 76cm
2015

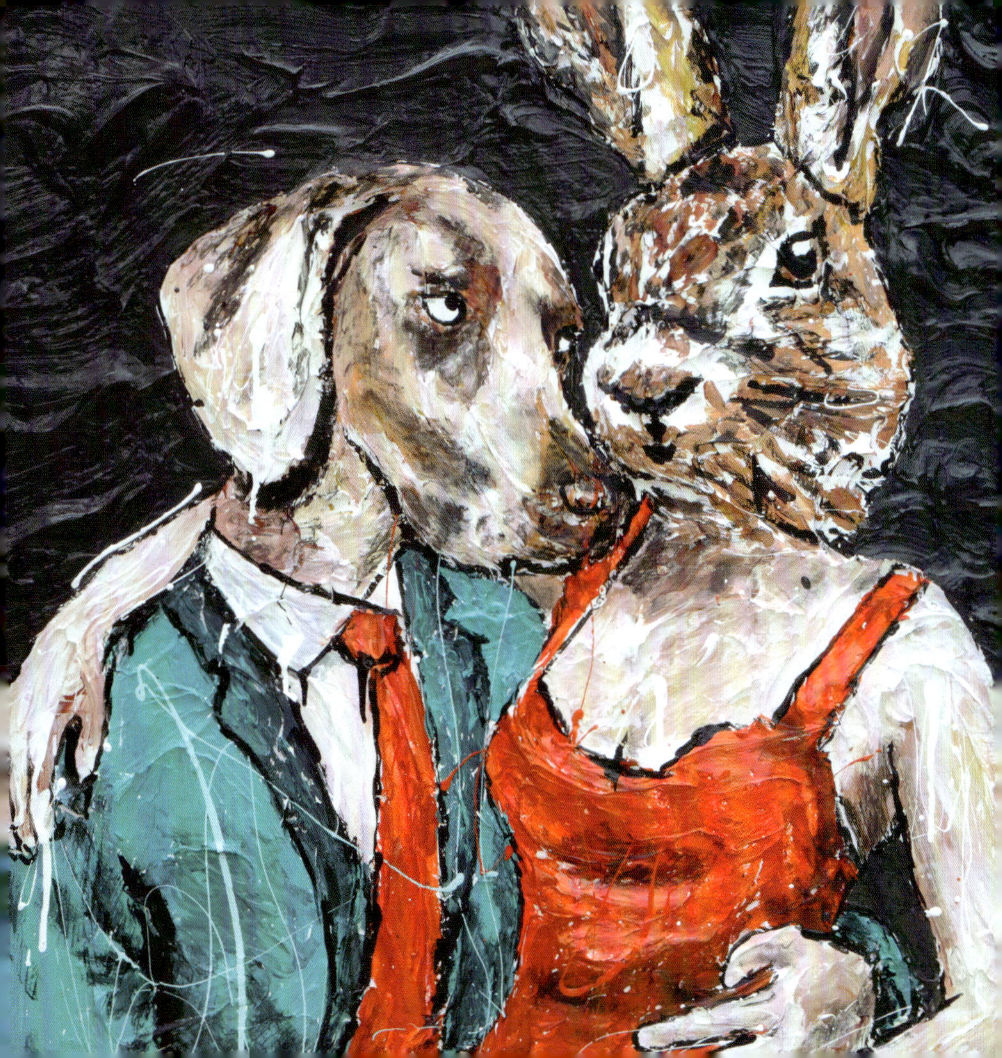

I want to be your last, not your first

She hoped this kiss would last forever
Bronze
28 x 26 x 17cm
2015

Photography by James Moffatt

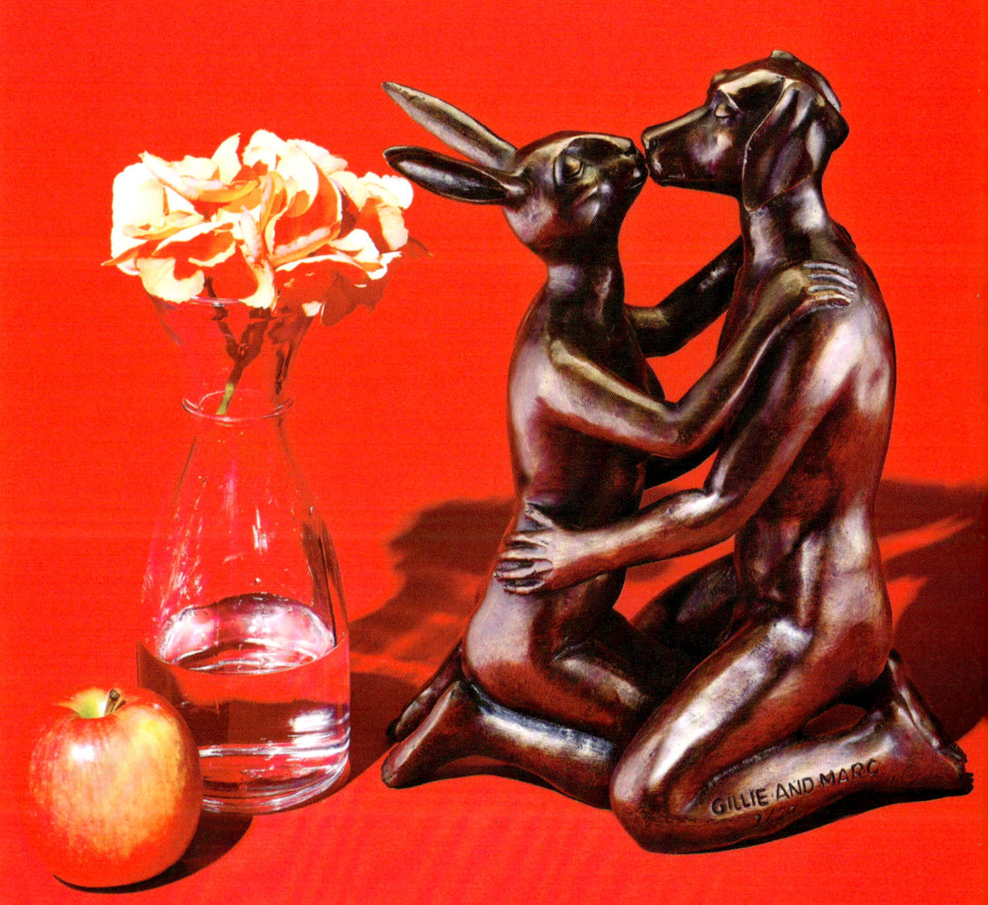
GILLIE AND MARC

Life is too short to wait for the sun to set

Happy Birthday Mr President xo
Permanently installed in Salamanca Square, Hobart
Bronze
Life-size
2014

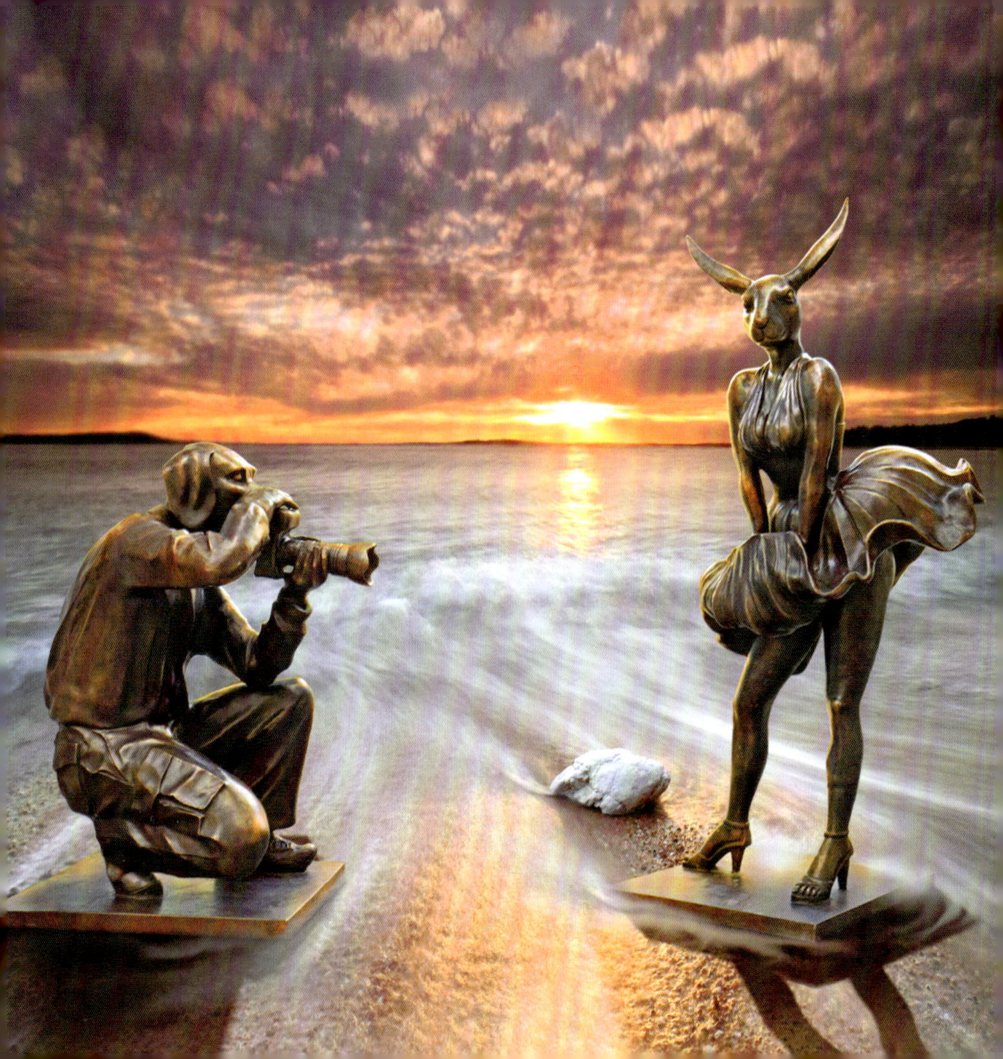

Nobody can be sad when riding a bicycle

They loved riding the streets of Paris
Mixed media on card
80 x 60cm
2015

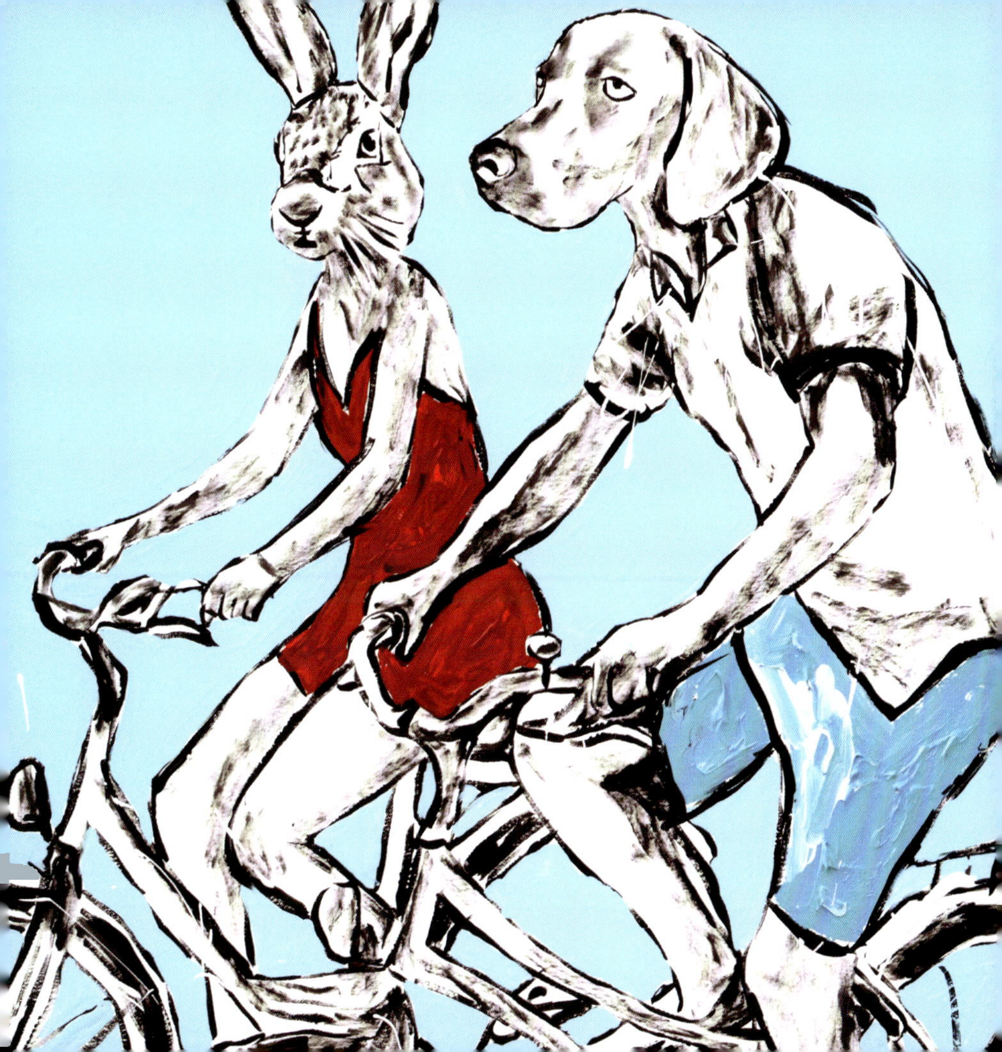

The quieter we are, the more we can hear

This was one of those moments in life when not a word was spoken but everything understood
Acrylic on canvas
198 x 152cm
2012

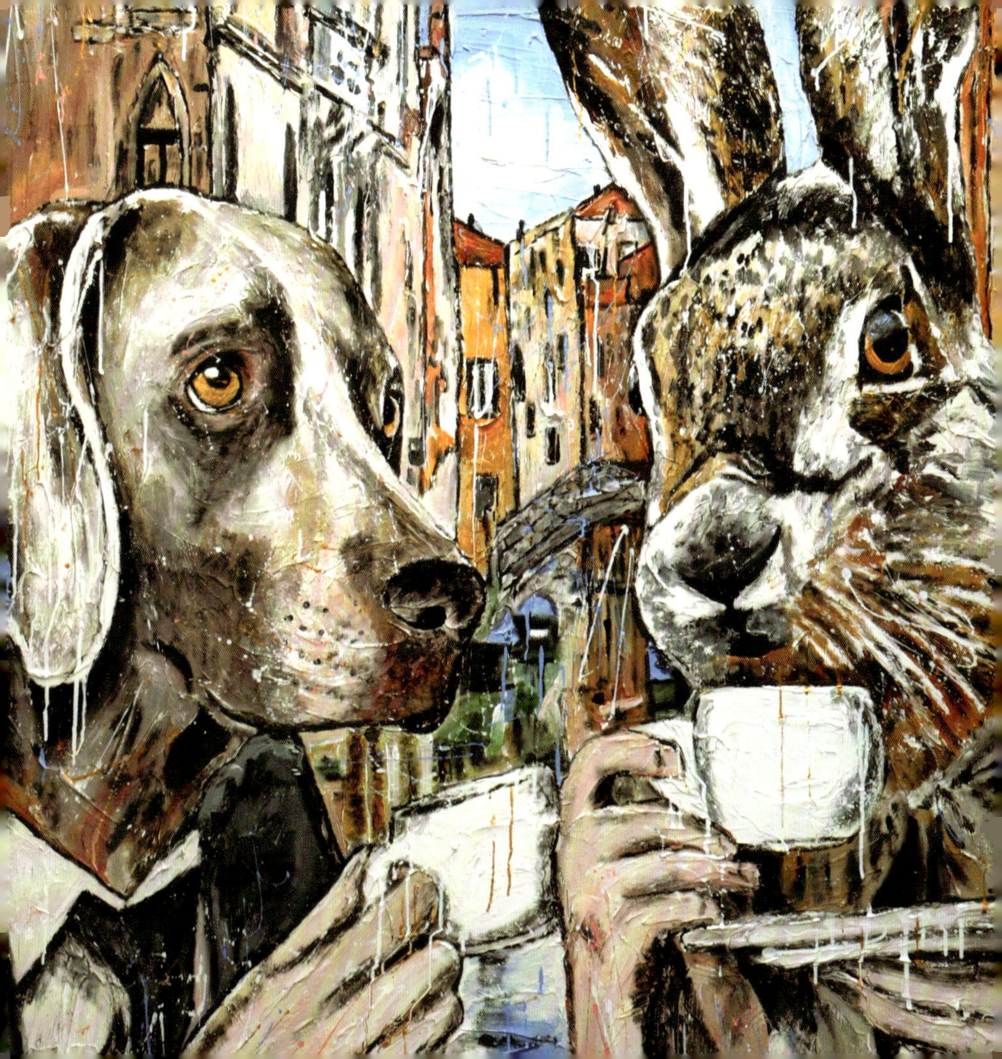

One bad apple doesn't make everybody bananas

Lolly Rabbitgirl and Dogman in Aston Martin
Clear Polyresin
19 x 32 x 14cm
2015

Photography by James Moffatt

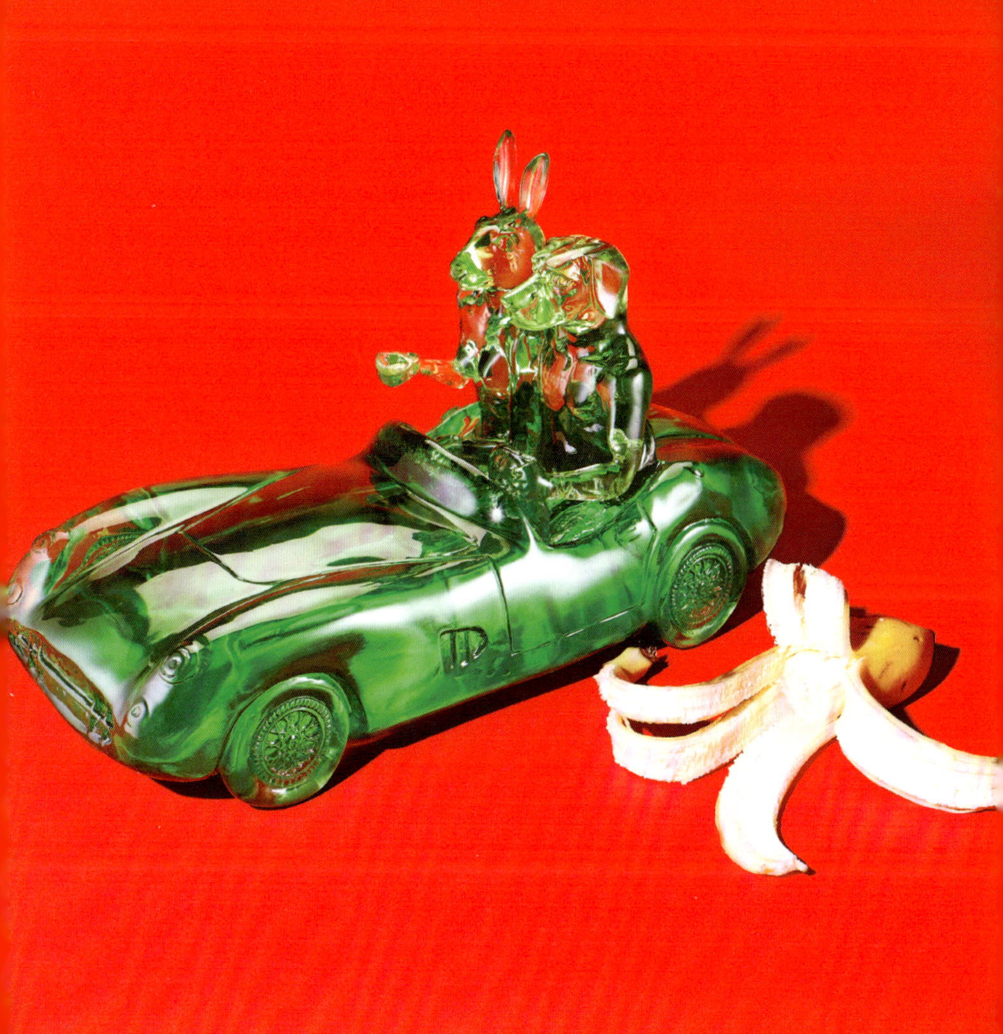

Beach therapy is the best therapy

Mini Riders
Bronze
42 x 68 x 30cm
2013

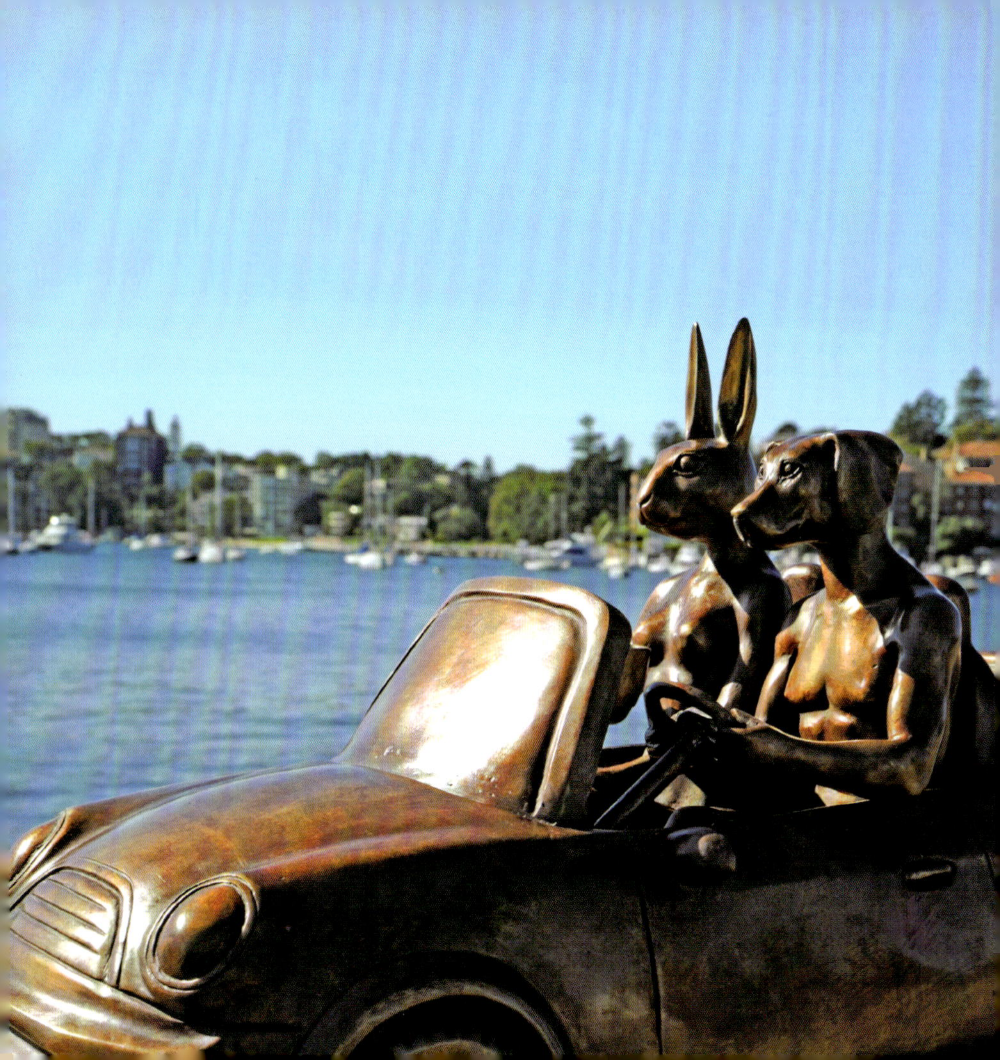

The best journeys answer questions you didn't even want answers to

He wanted to take her somewhere special, but where?
Mixed media on card
80 x 60cm
2015

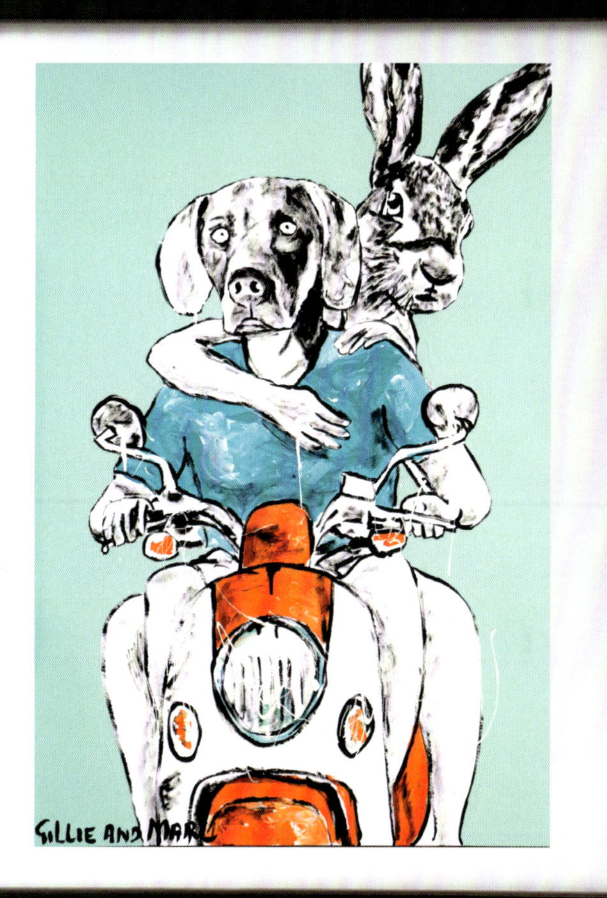
GILLIE AND MARC

Don't think. Let's just run with it and see where we end up

Baby you can ride my car, baby it will take you far, but just don't scratch it!!
Acrylic on canvas
120 x 120cm
2012

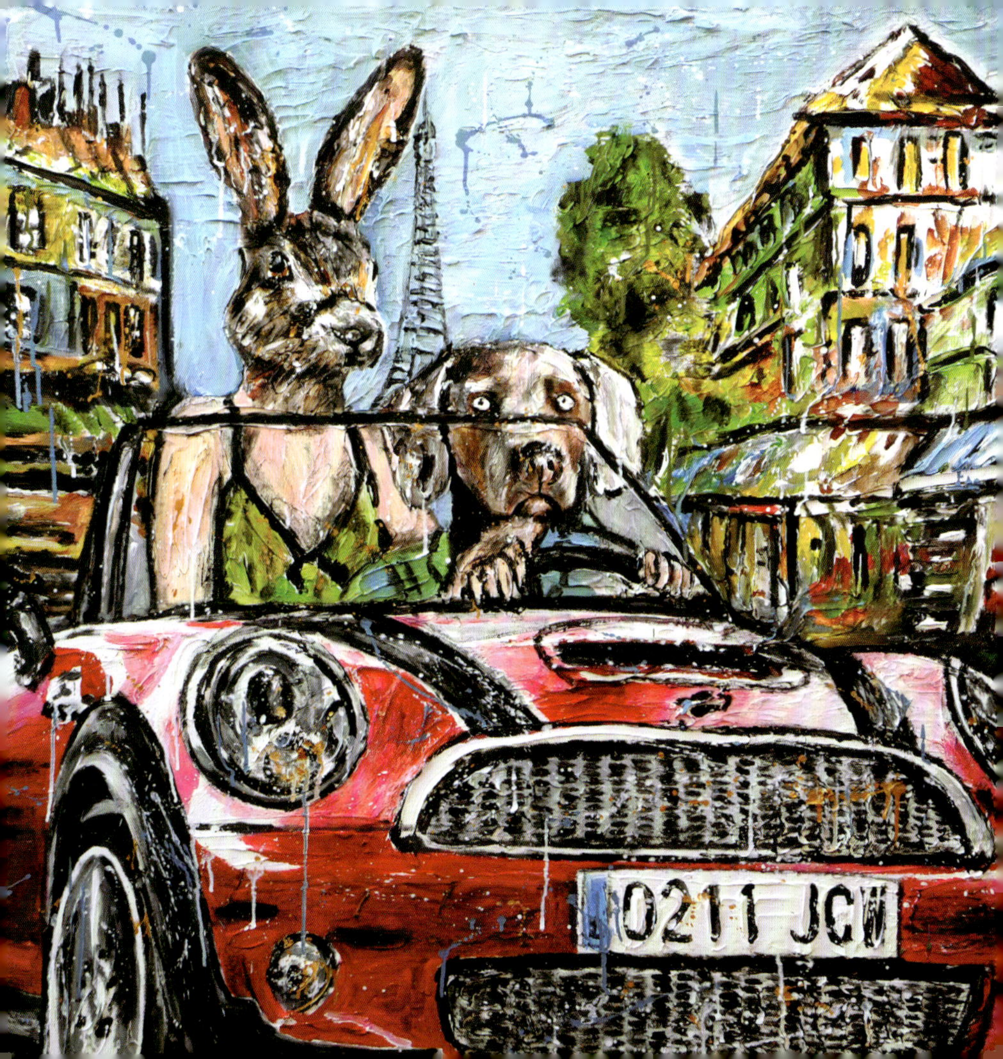
O211 JCW

Getting lost helps you find yourself

Right: *Lost Dog*
Left: *Lost Rabbit*
Fibreglass and 2pak paint
67cm and 89cm high
2014

Photography by James Moffatt

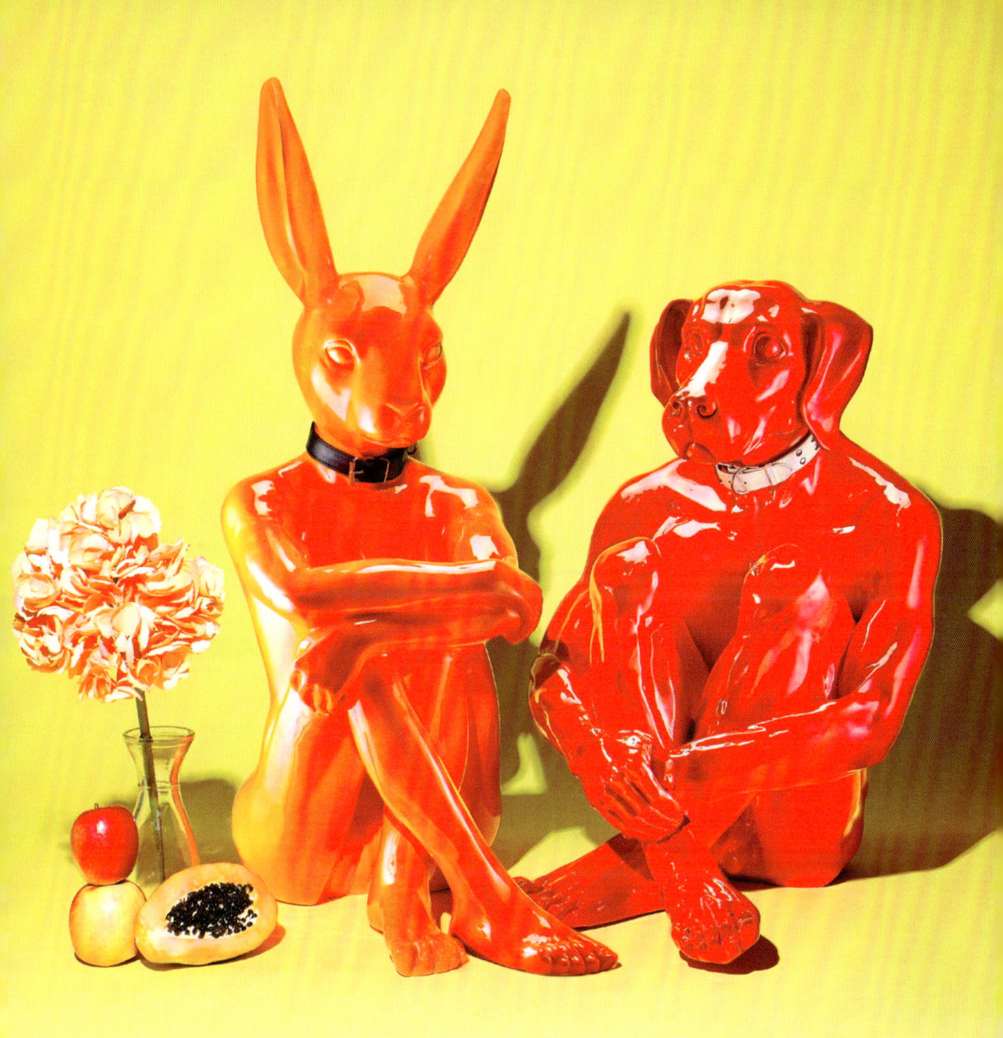

Sometimes we just need to change shells and do something new

The Crab Riders
Exhibited at Woolloomooloo Wharf, Sydney
Bronze
245cm high
2013

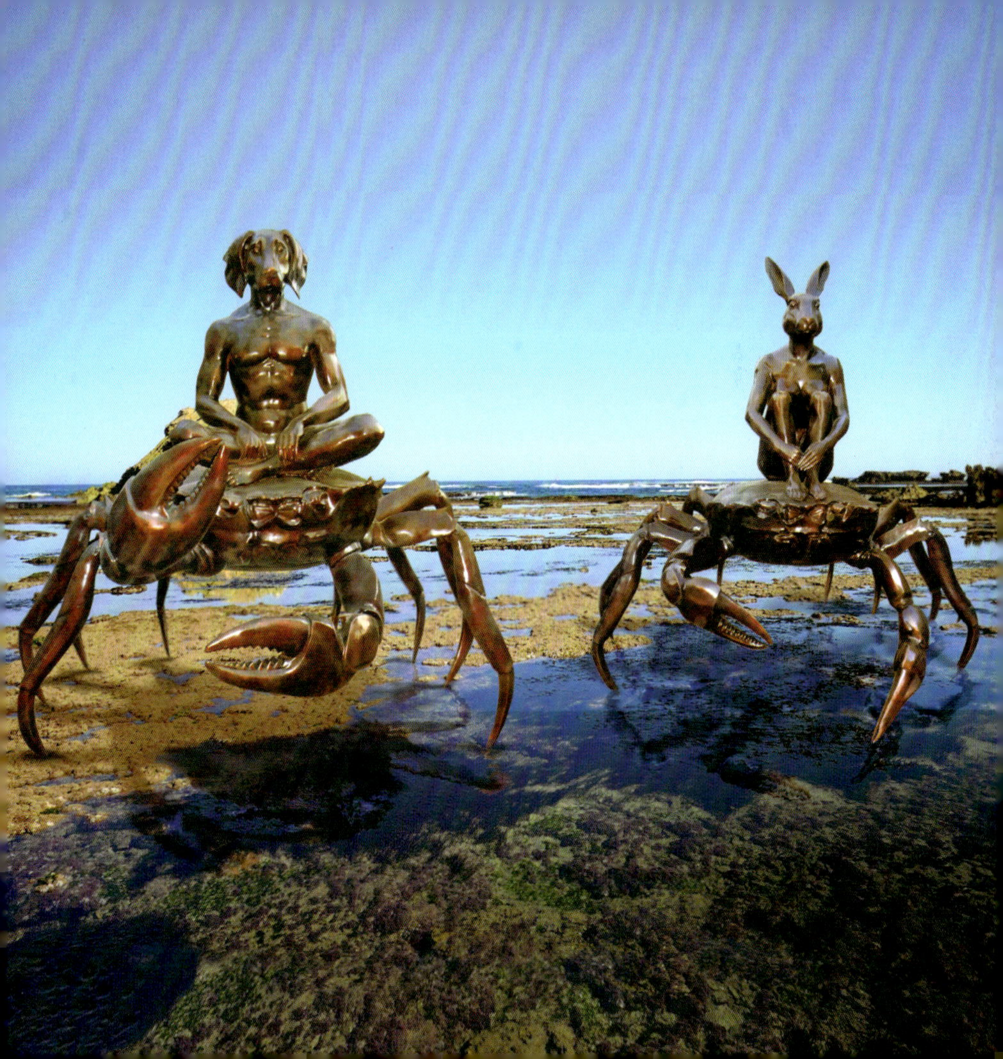

The best paths in life are the unfamiliar ones

Driving along Venice's canals to have
Tiramisù at their favourite trattoria
Acrylic on board
91 x 91cm
2015

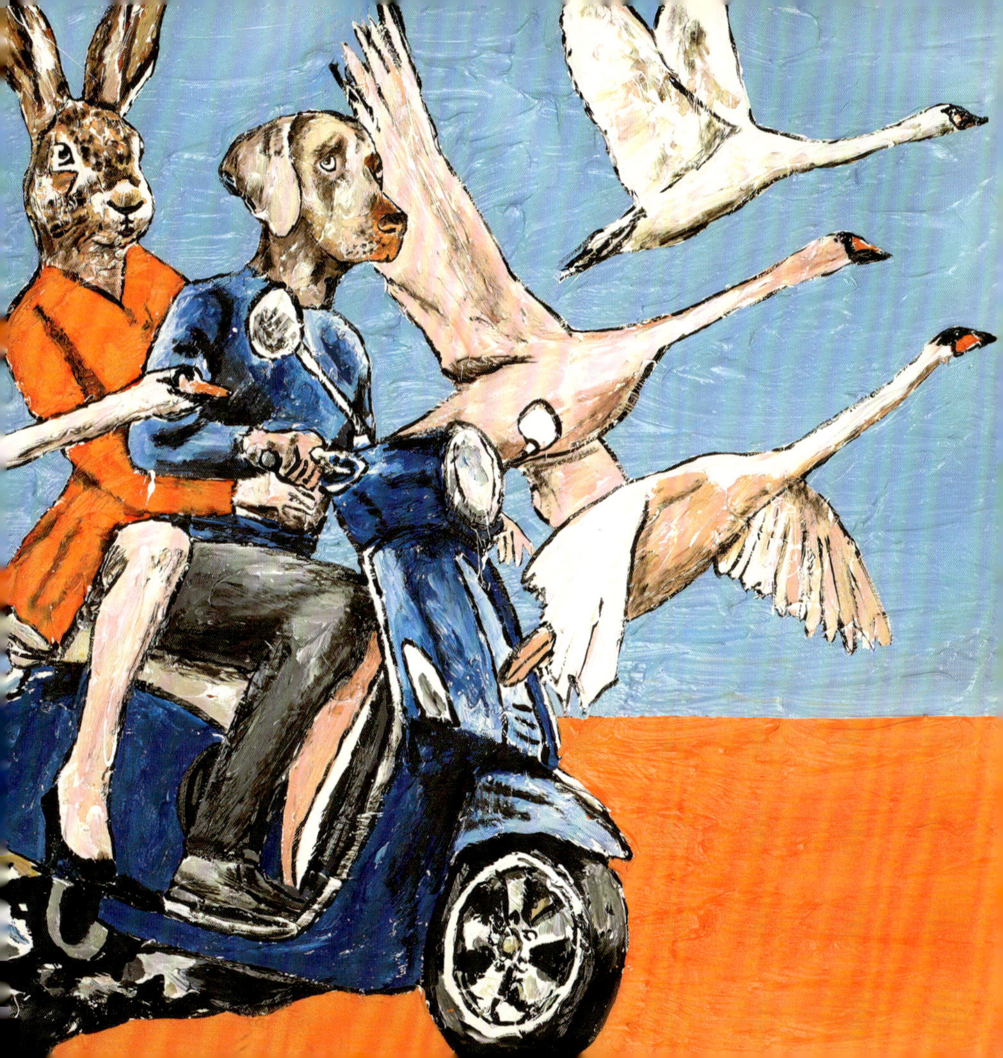

A cup of coffee shared is happiness tasted and time well spent

They love their first cup and their second, third etc
Mixed media on card
80 x 60cm
2015

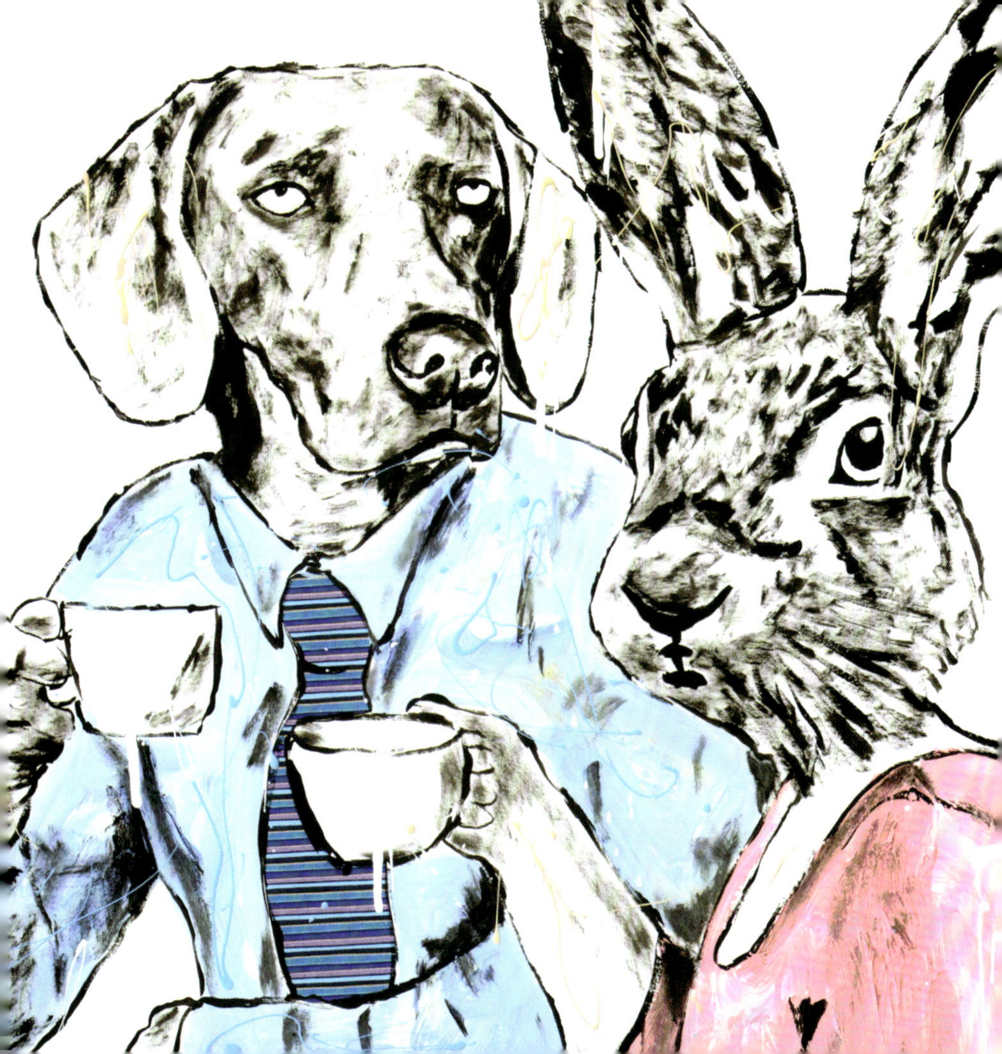

When life gives you lemons, you can make more than just lemonade

Right: *Mini Dogman*
Left: *Mini Rabbitgirl*
Polyresin
18.5 and 26.5cm high
2015

Photography by James Moffatt

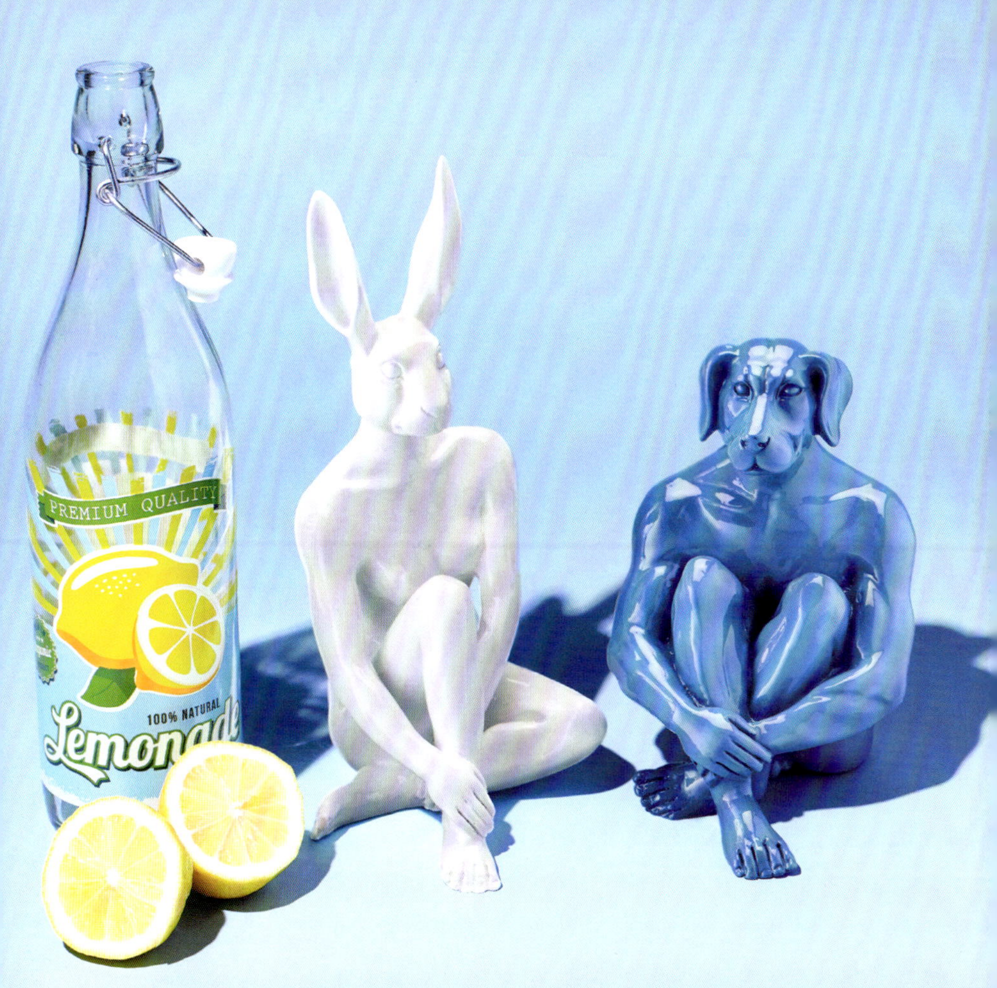
PREMIUM QUALITY
100% NATURAL
Lemonade

Together, everybody achieves more

Run for your life
Purchased by Wonderment Walk Victoria and gifted to La Trobe University, Melbourne
Bronze
Life-size
2014

Photography by William Watt

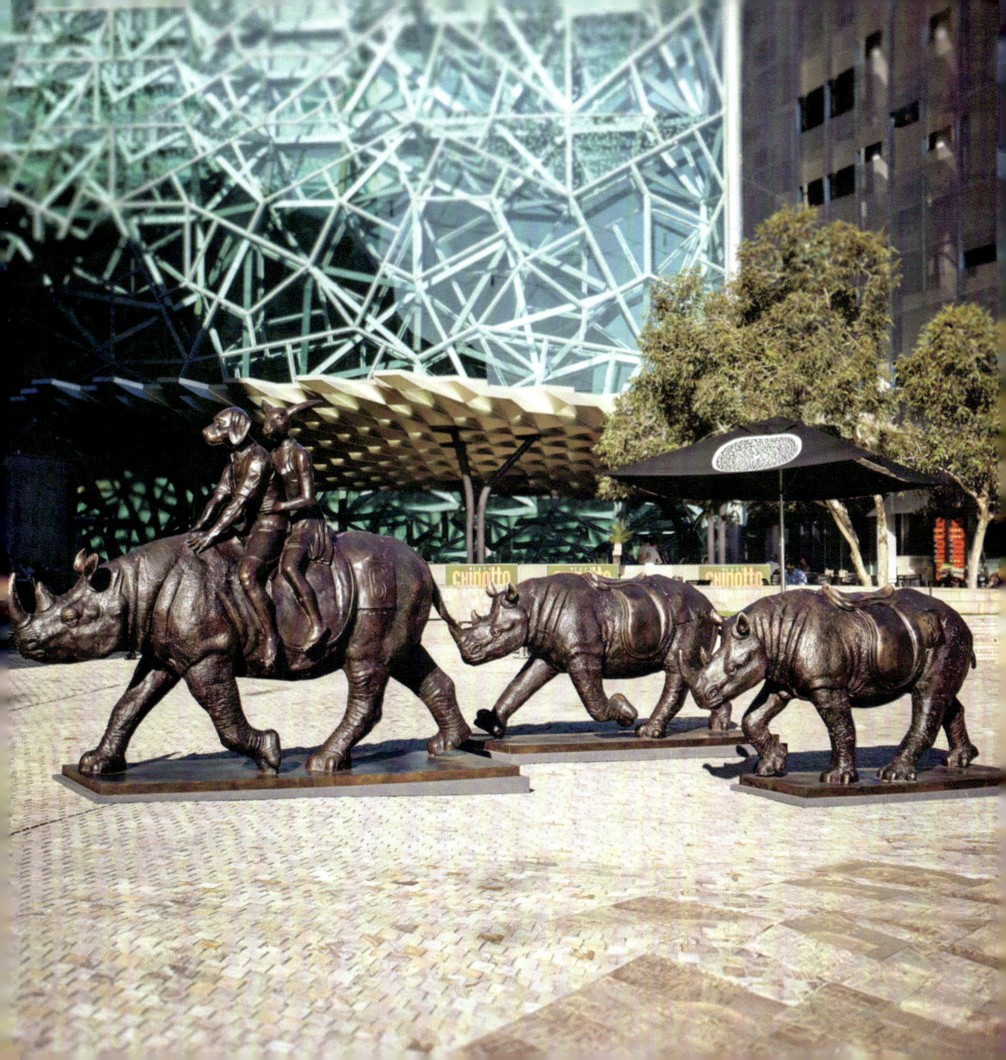
chinotto
chinotto

In our dreams, we ride wild horses

They knew life was up and down but
that's what made the ride special
Acrylic on canvas
120 x 120cm
2015

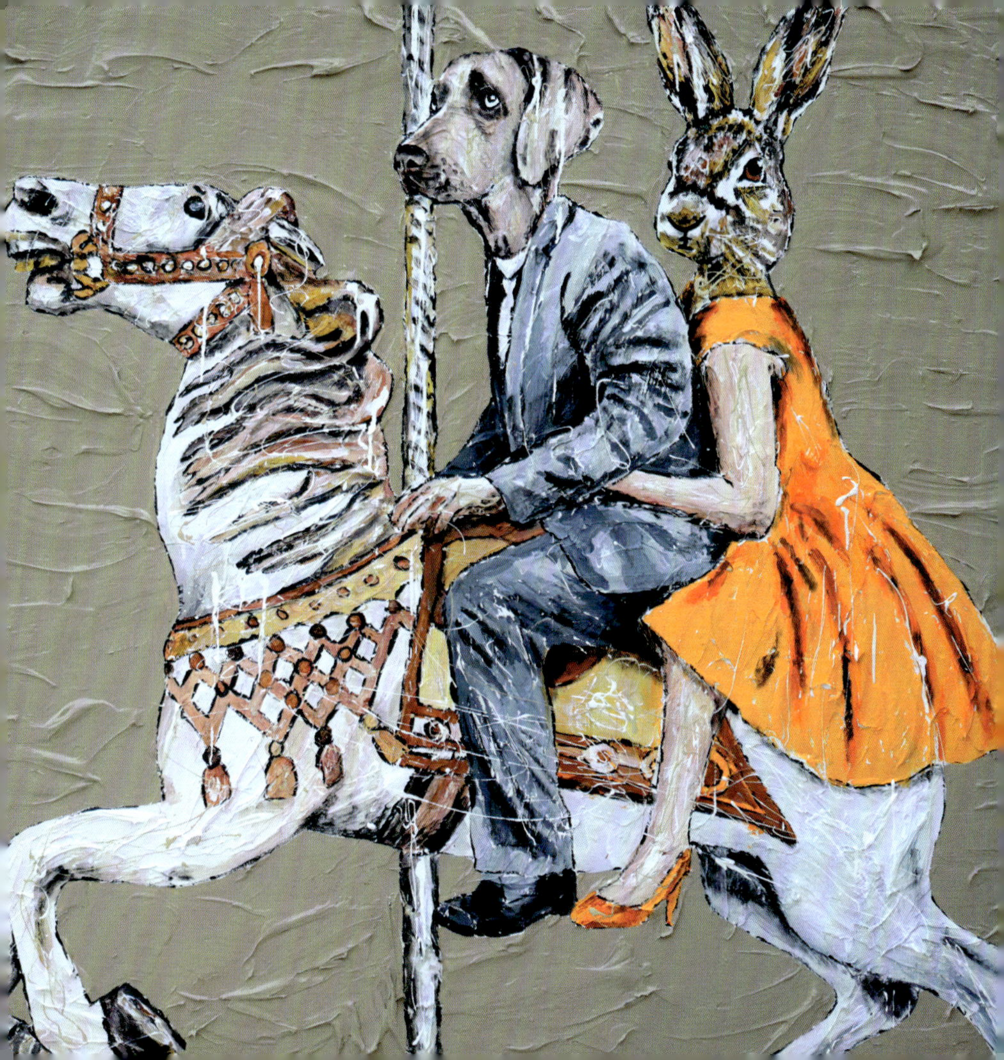

Ride the wave you're given; it might be a long time until the next one comes

Lolly Surfers
Polyresin
37 x 40 x 8.5cm
2015

Photography by James Moffatt

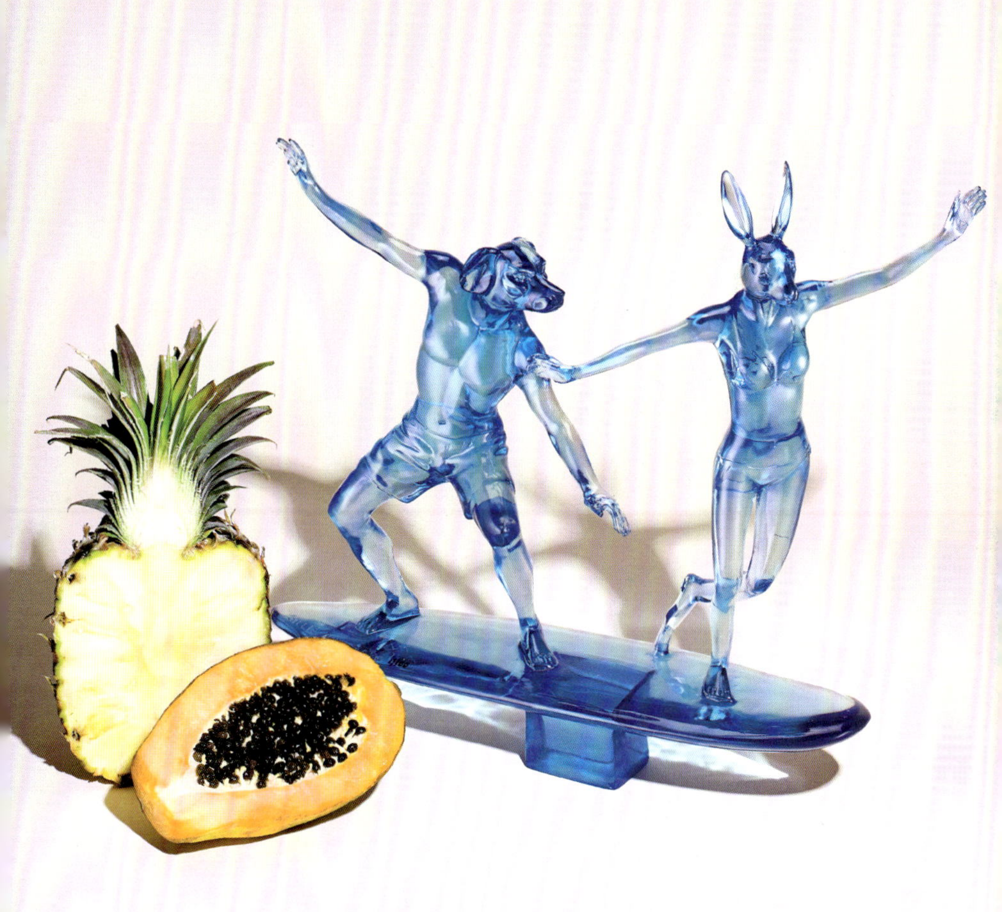

I’m warm. You’re cold.
Let’s cuddle

Rome in August was better than any chocolate
Acrylic on board
91 x 91cm
2014

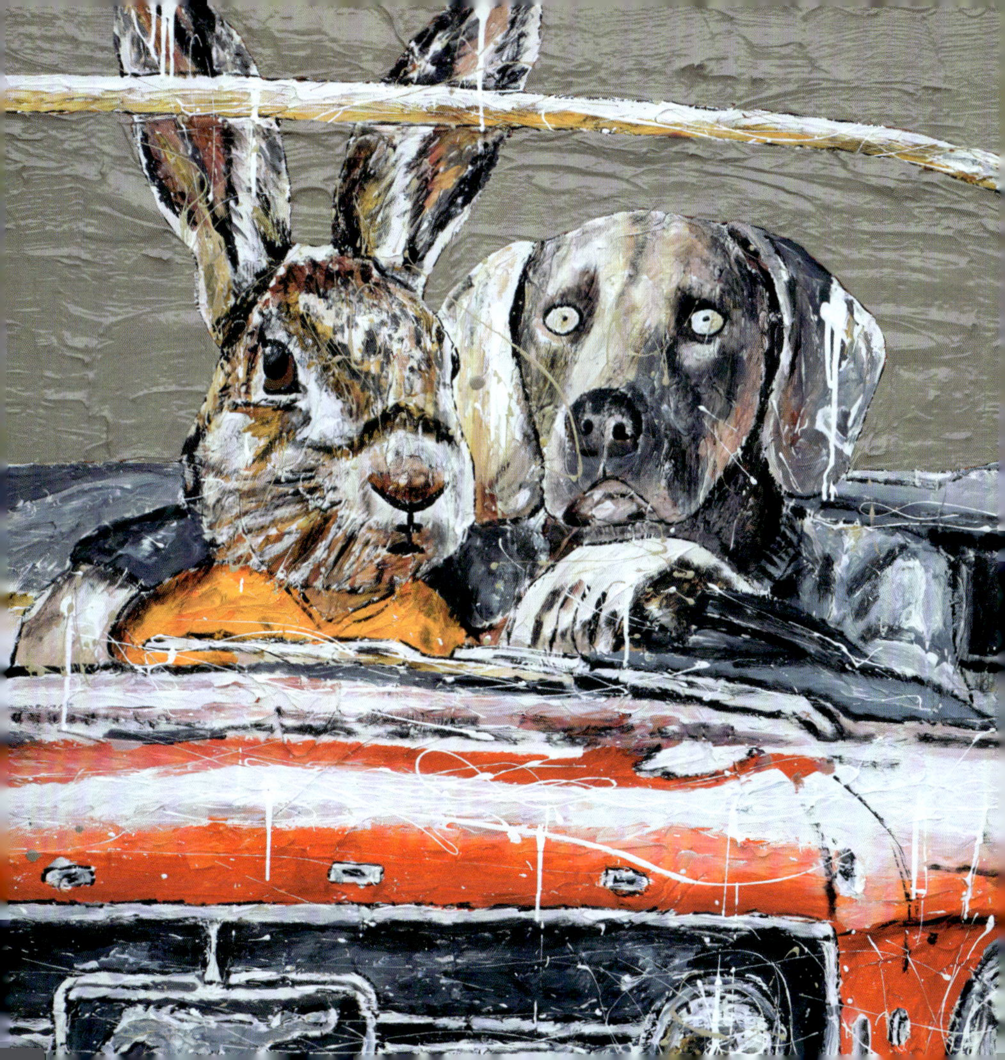

We'll get there because of our differences, not in spite of them

Right: *The travellers have arrived*
Centre: *They loved riding together in Paris*
Left: *They were the authentic Vespa riders*
Bronze
23cm high
2015

Photography by James Moffatt

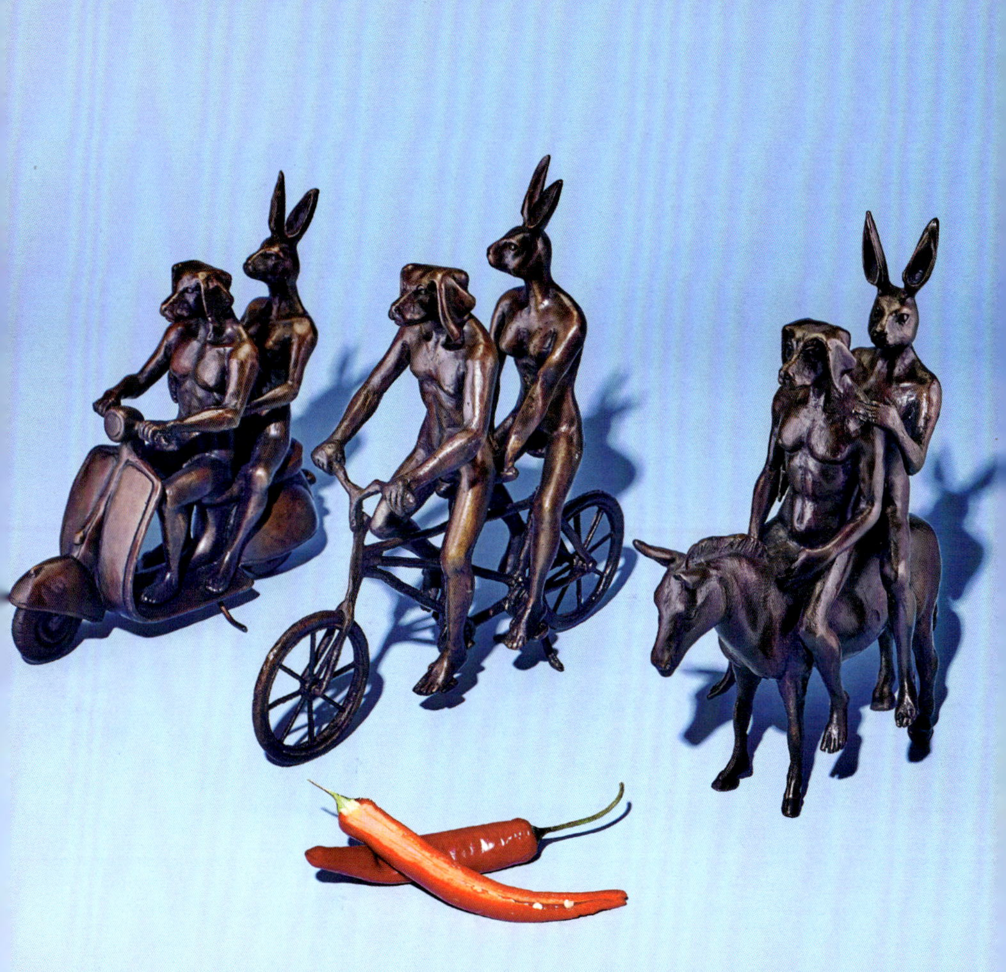

It’s not the destination anymore.
It’s the ride

He said to her, let’s ride like the wind
Acrylic on canvas
120 x 120cm
2014

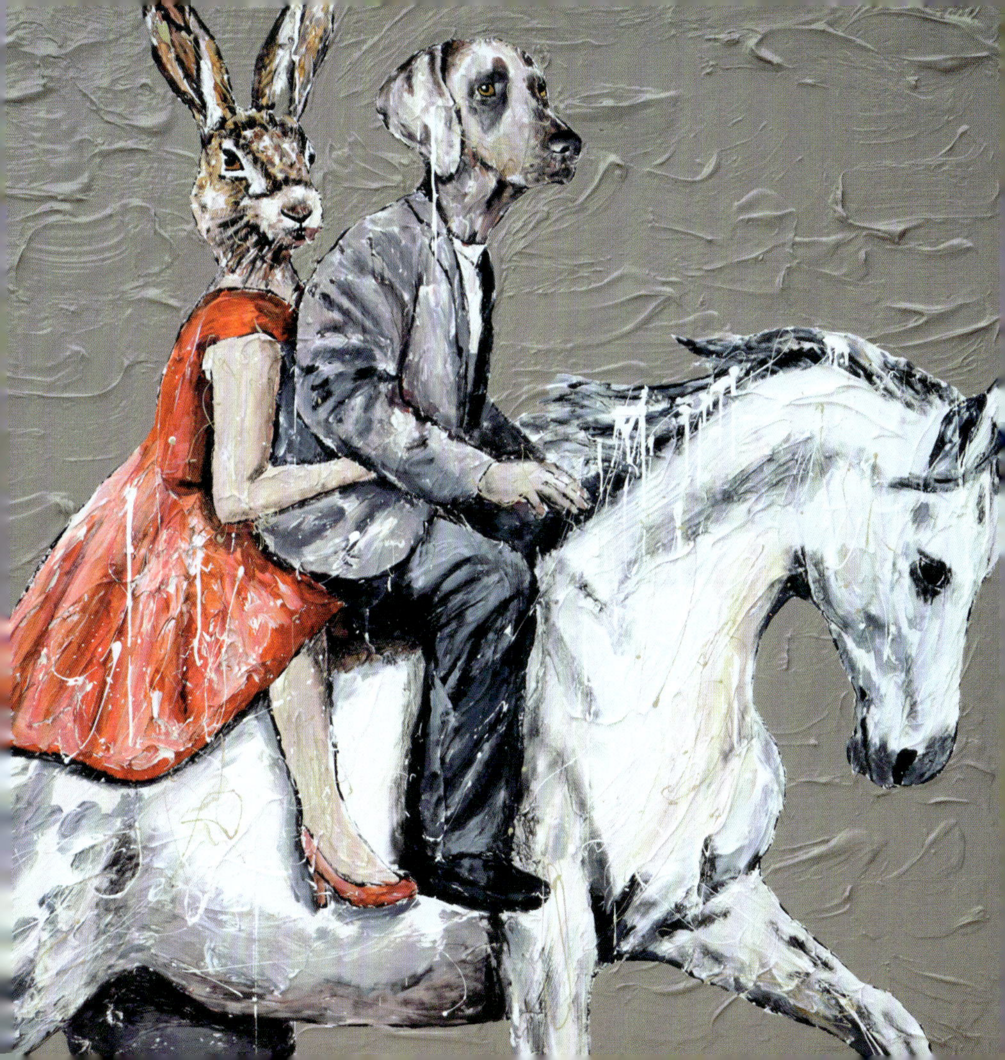

We don't exist to follow rules

He told her he would wait for her forever
... unless someone hotter came along
Acrylic on canvas
76 x 76cm
2015

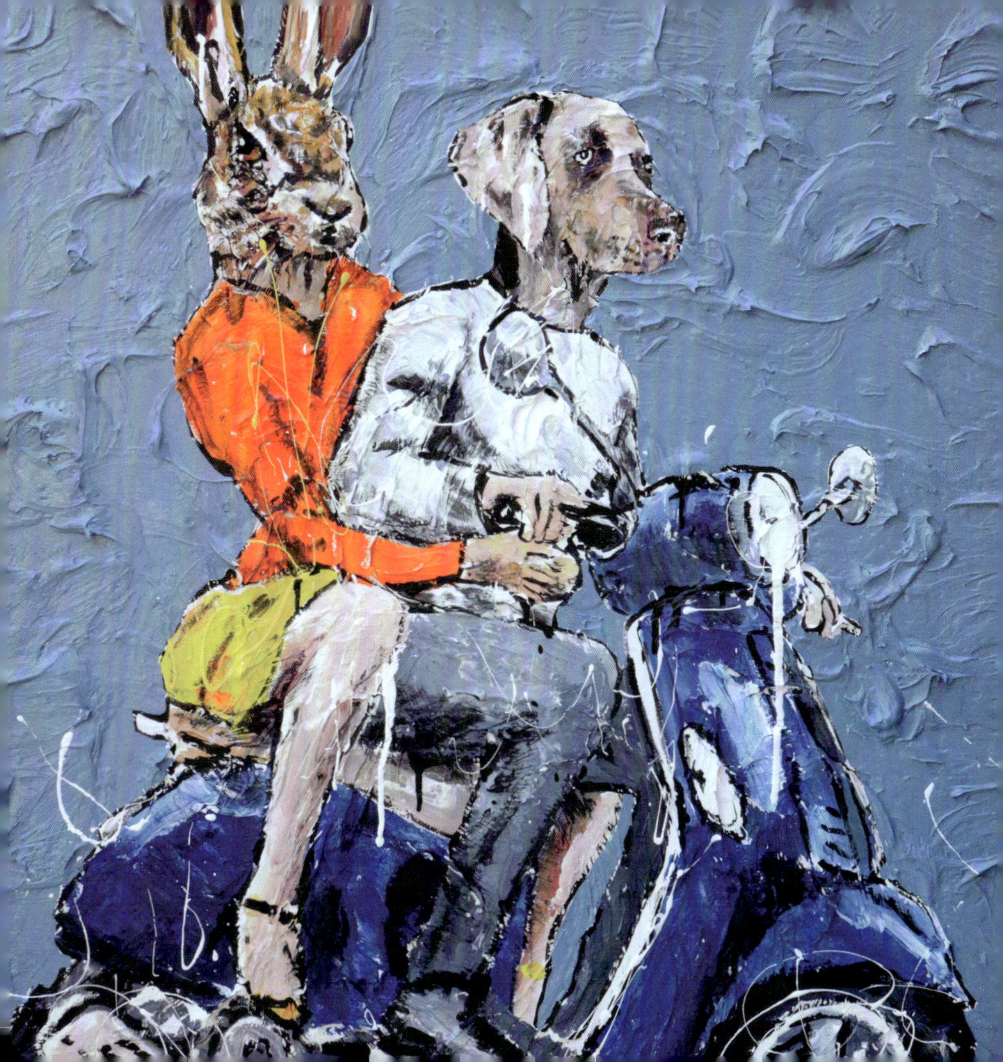

Simplicity and complexity need one another

Right: *Lolly Dogman*
Left: *Lolly Rabbitgirl*
Polyresin
18.5 and 26.5cm high
2015

Photography by James Moffatt

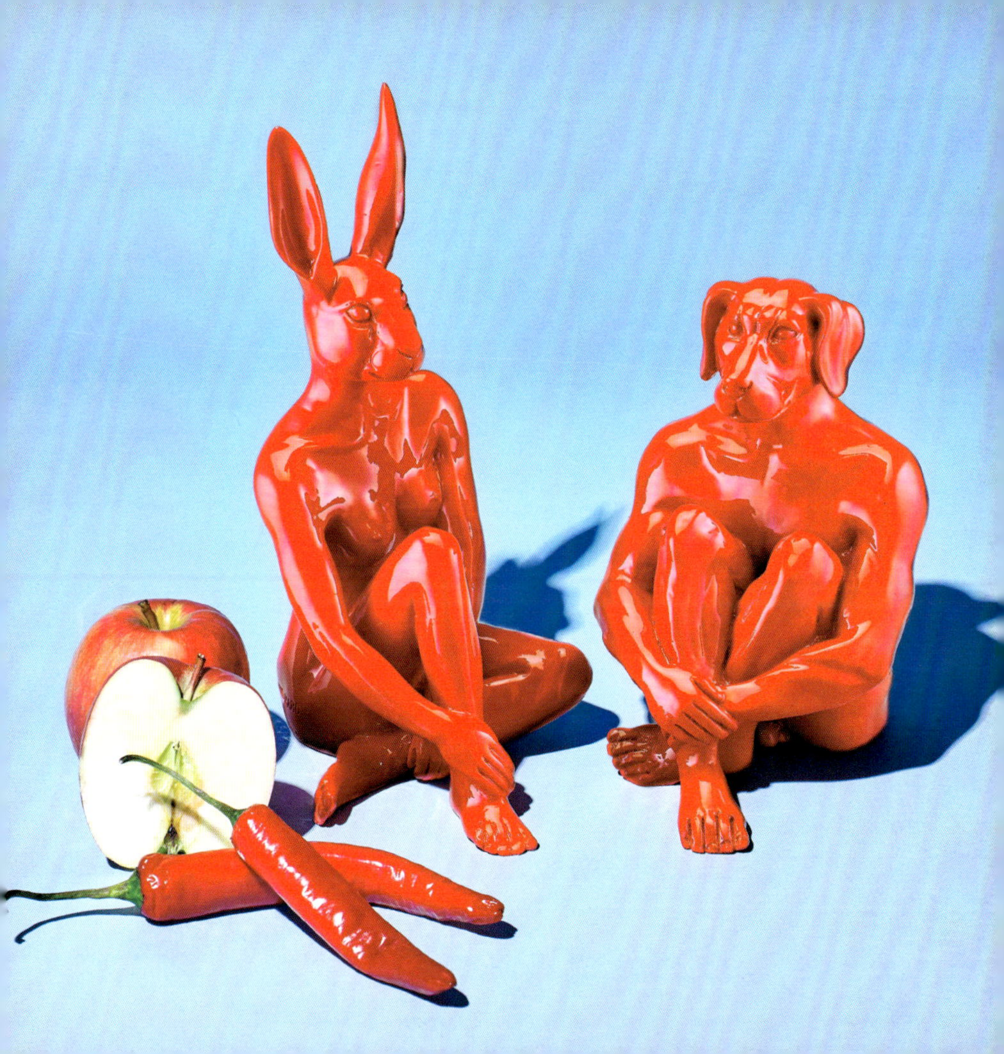

Opposites attract, but like minds last

Right: *Lolly Dogman*
Left: *Lolly Rabbitgirl*
Clear Polyresin
35 and 45cm high
2014

Photography by James Moffatt

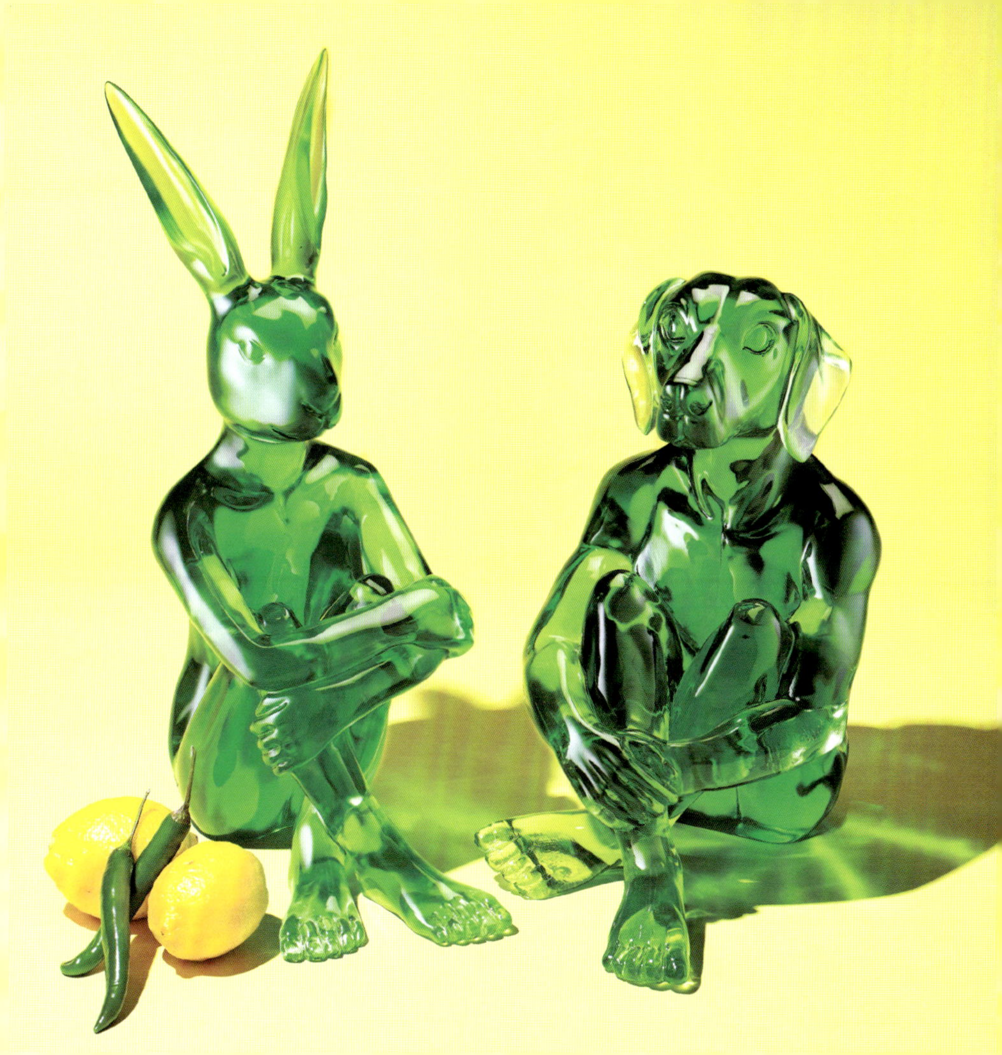

Don't be afraid to be a flamingo among a flock of pigeons

He loved giving her the unexpected and that's what she expected him to do
Acrylic on canvas
150 x 150cm
2015

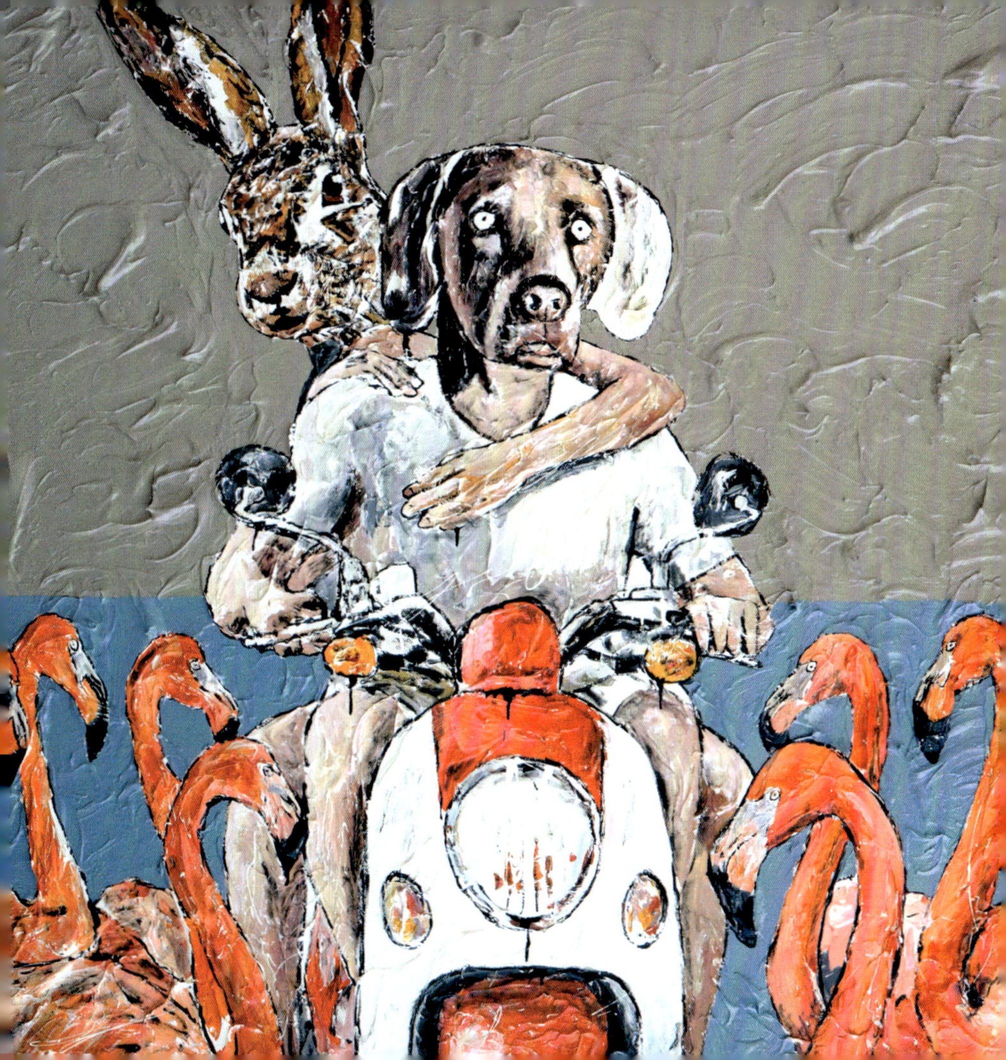

When words fail you, let the music speak

Right: *He lived to the beat of his drum*
Left: *She played jazz during the week and classical on the weekend*
Bronze
32 and 37cm high
2015

Photography by James Moffatt

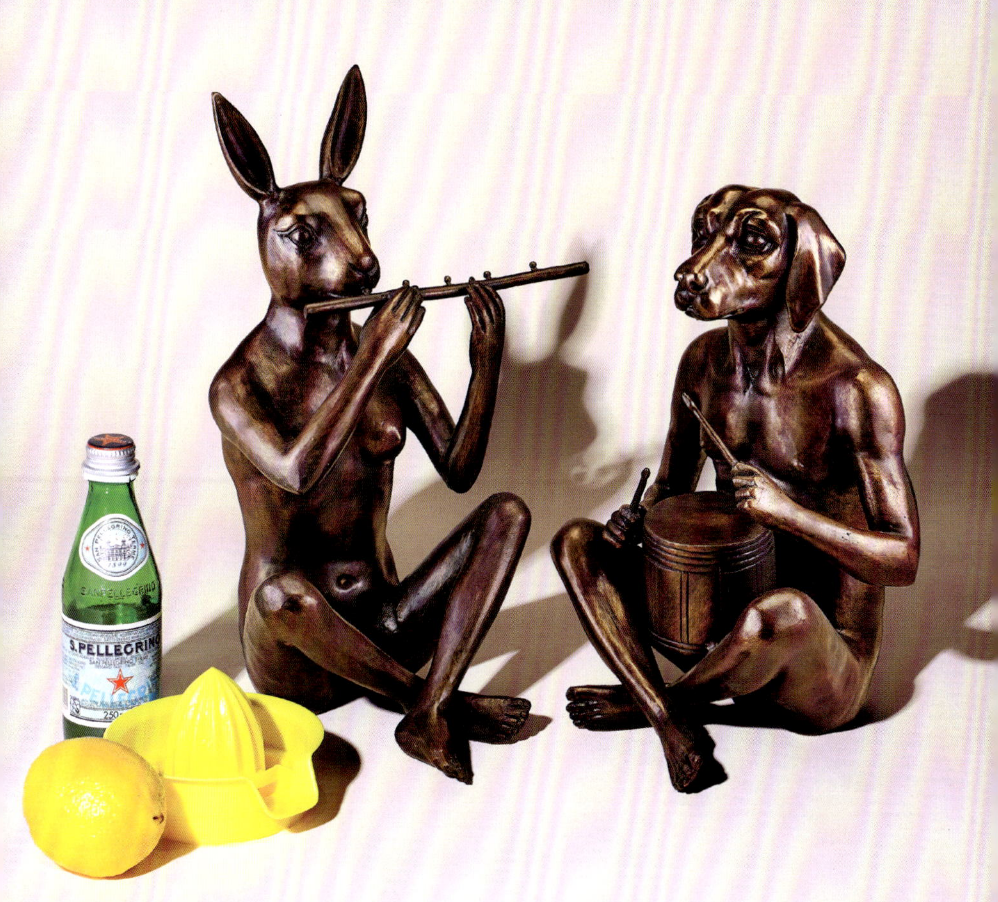
SANPELLEGRINO
S.PELLEGRINO

Nothing is better than a wild goose chase

They were excited to be taken somewhere they had never been
Acrylic on canvas
120 x 240cm
2015

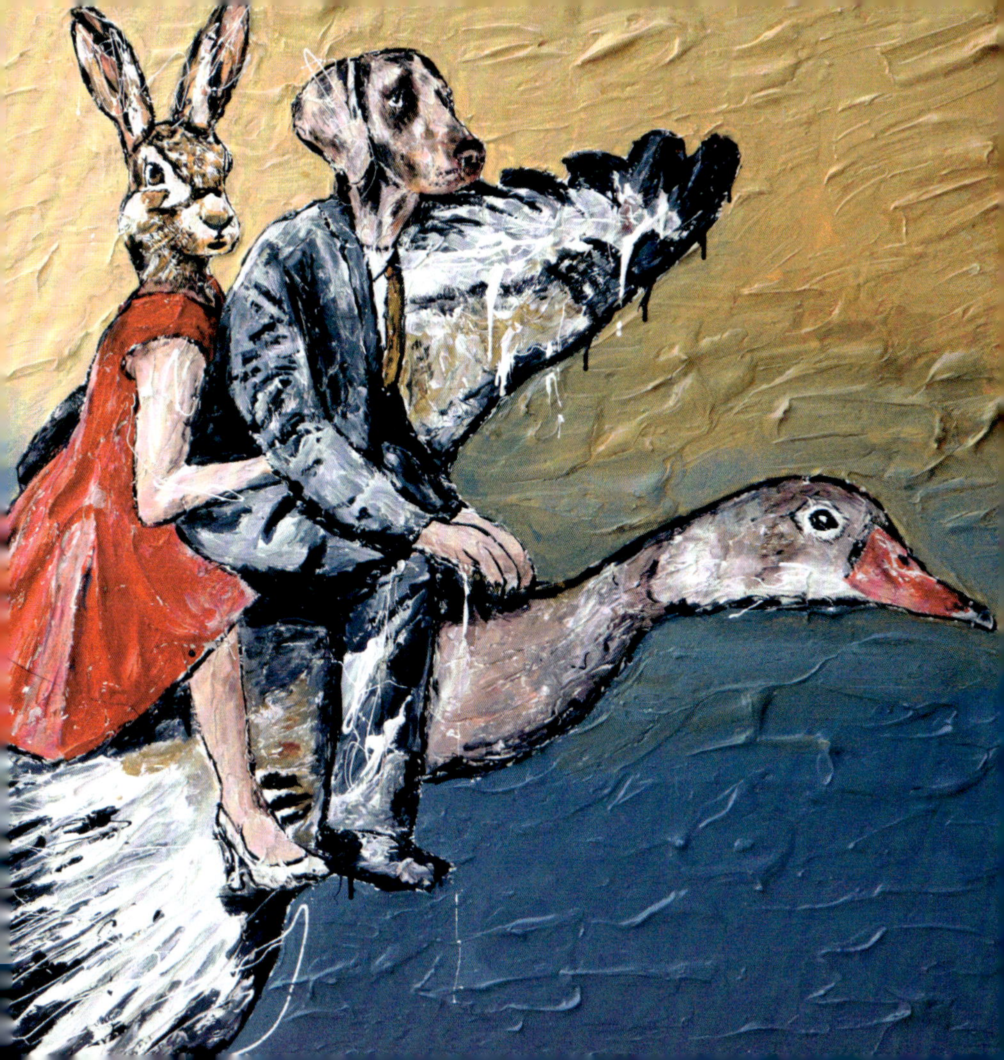

Be the type of leader you would follow

Scooter Riders
Bronze
56 x 40 x 14cm
2012

Photography by James Moffatt

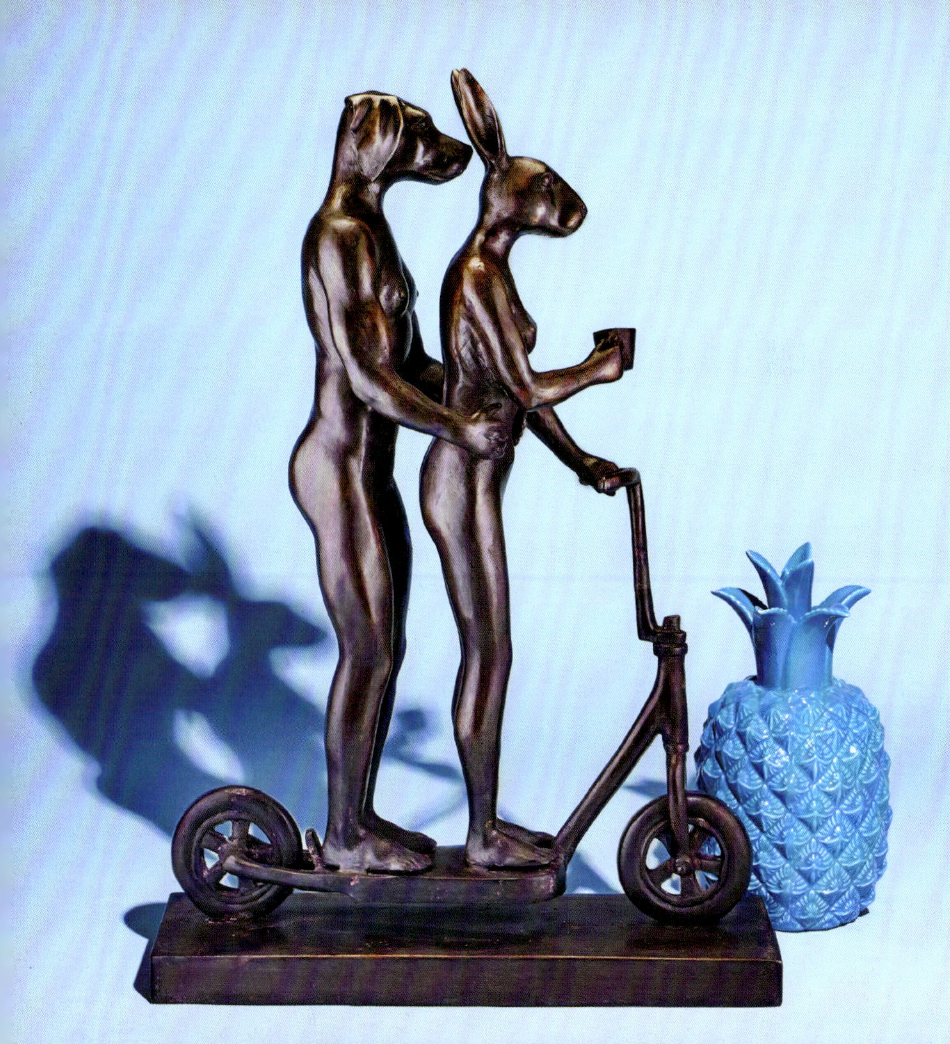

Just like the sun, we spread warmth just by being ourselves

Coffee for two in Bondi
Acrylic on canvas
90 x 60cm
2013

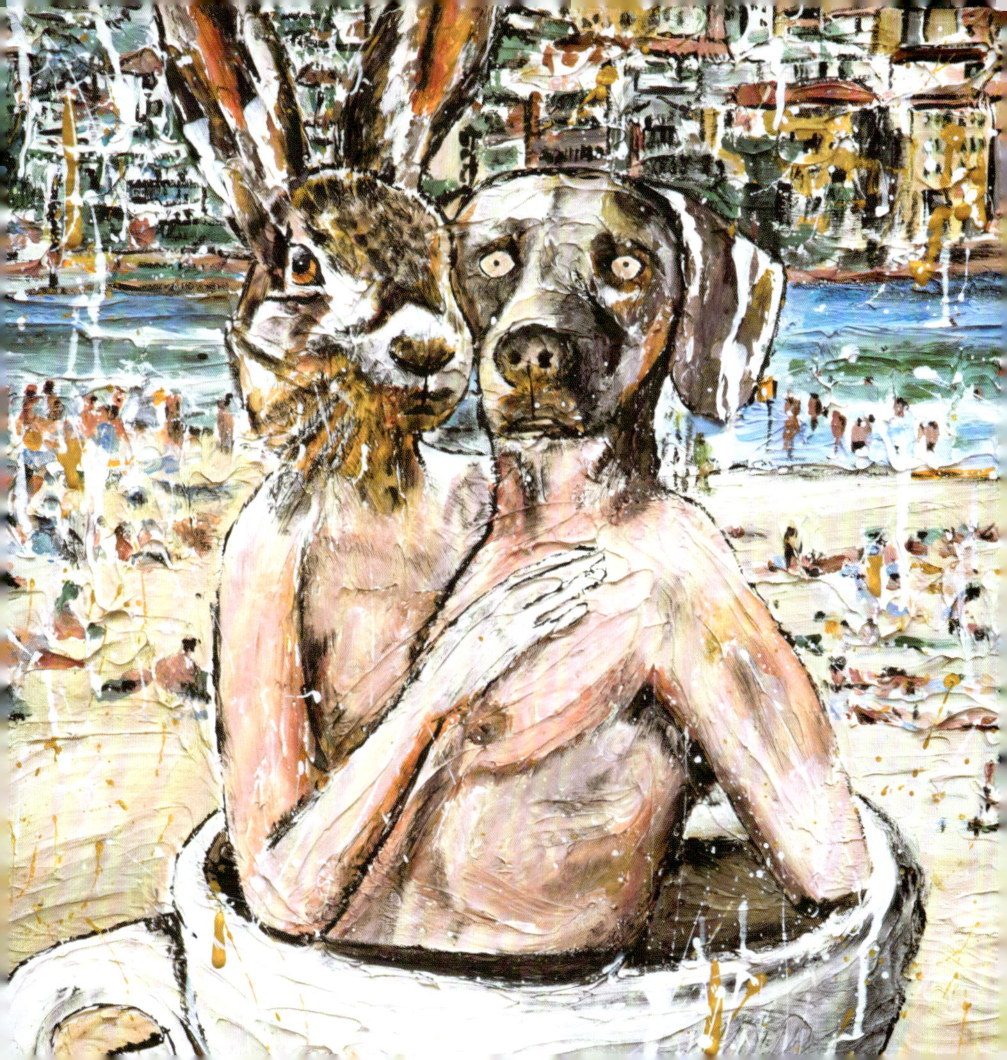

Leave your phone at home.
Go outside. Meet someone new

Right: *She thought a bird and coffee in the hand is better than just a bird*
Left: *He thought the early bird gets the coffee*
Bronze
60 and 50cm high
2014

Photography by Jessie Schattner

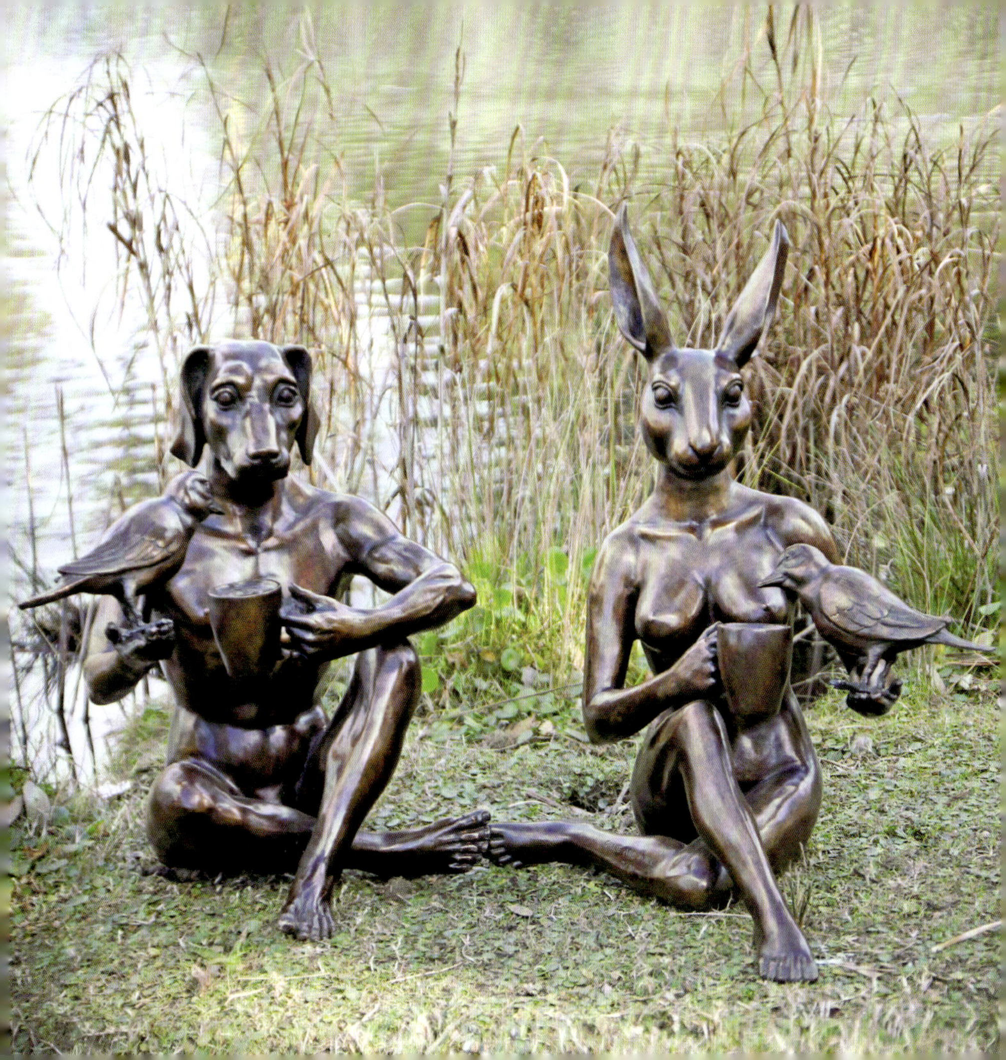

Paintings are best left to speak for themselves

She wondered if she bought the painting if it would rocket in price
Acrylic on canvas
120 x 90cm
2015

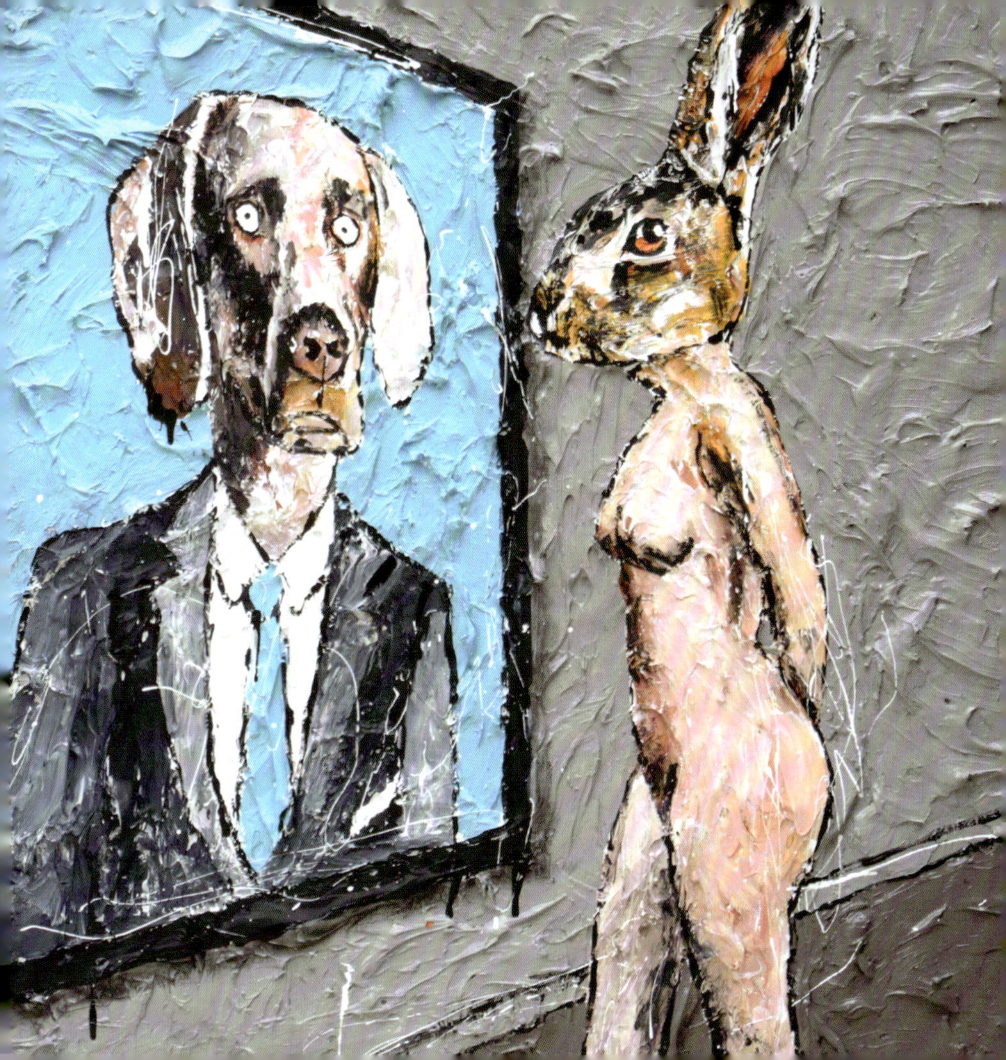

You're allowed to hit refresh as many times as you want

Right: *Mini lolly Dogman*
Left: *Mini lolly Rabbitgirl*
Clear Polyresin
18.5 and 26.5cm high
2015

Photography by James Moffatt

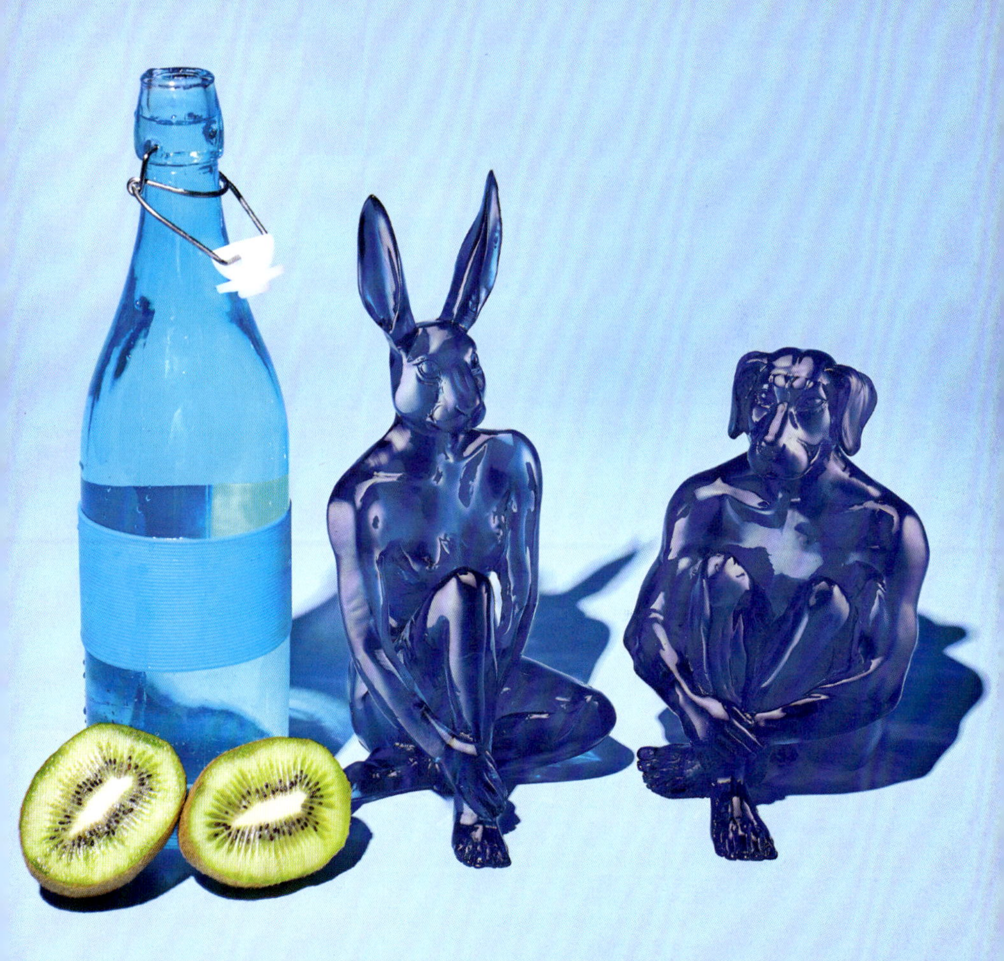

We have our wings.
All we need to do is take flight

She thought they were all birds of a feather so they stuck together
Acrylic on board
120 x 90cm
2015

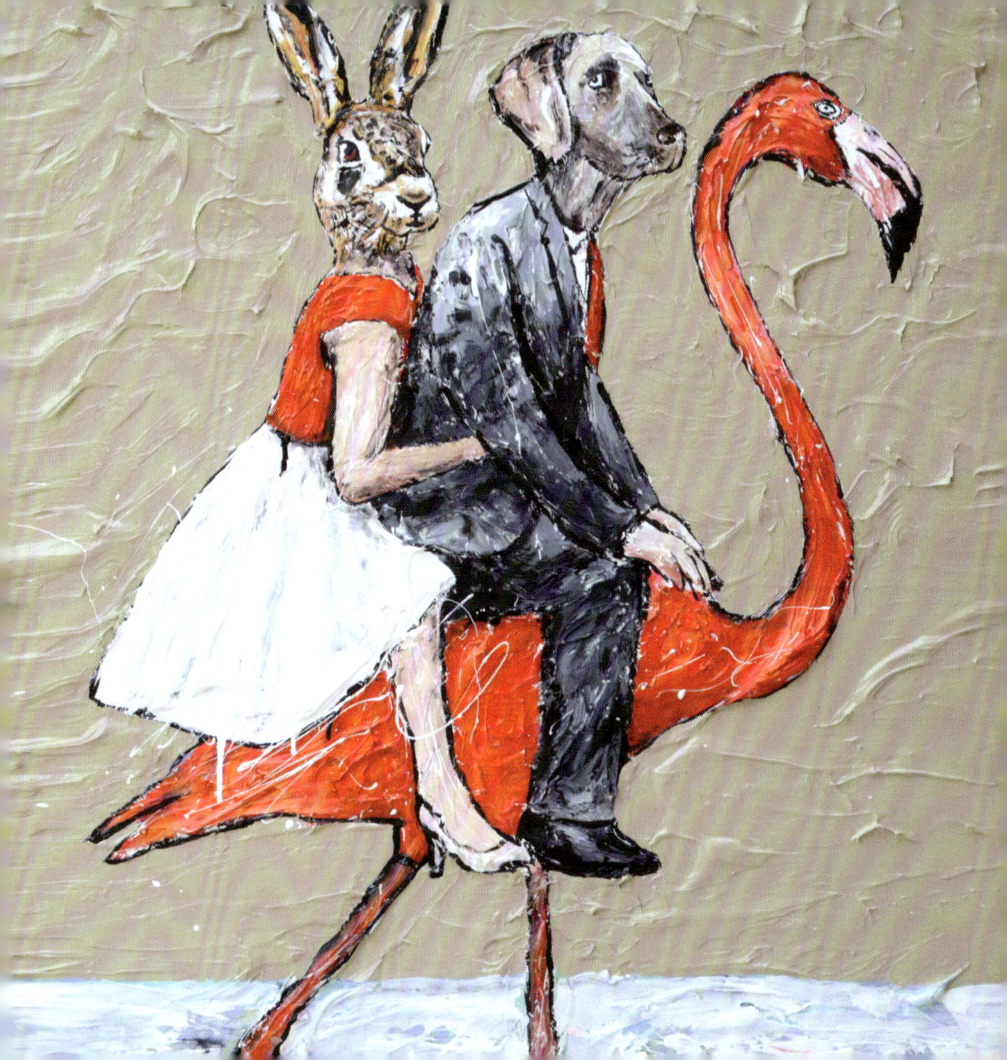

When you stop struggling, you float

He was seasick but she was so happy so he smiled and kept rowing
Bronze
42 x 52 x 50cm
2015

Photography by James Moffatt

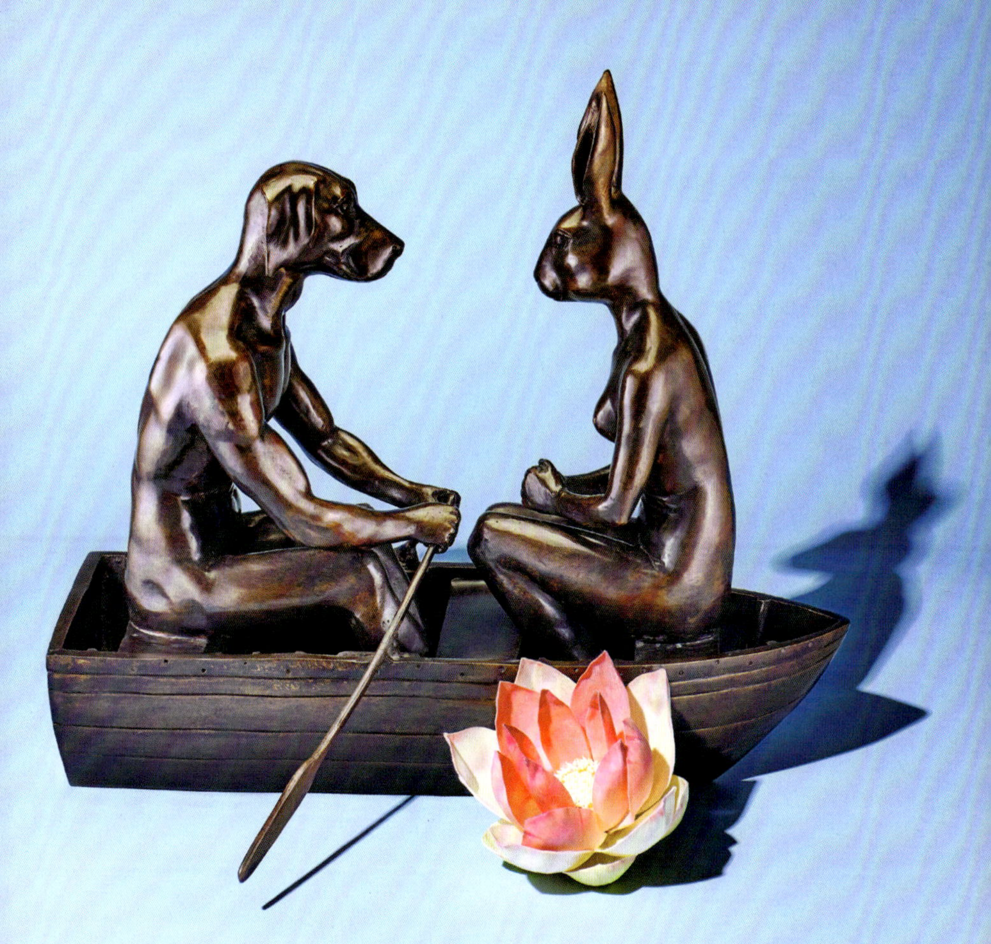

But first, we need coffee

Large Coffee Drinkers
Double Bay, Sydney
Bronze
200cm high
2013

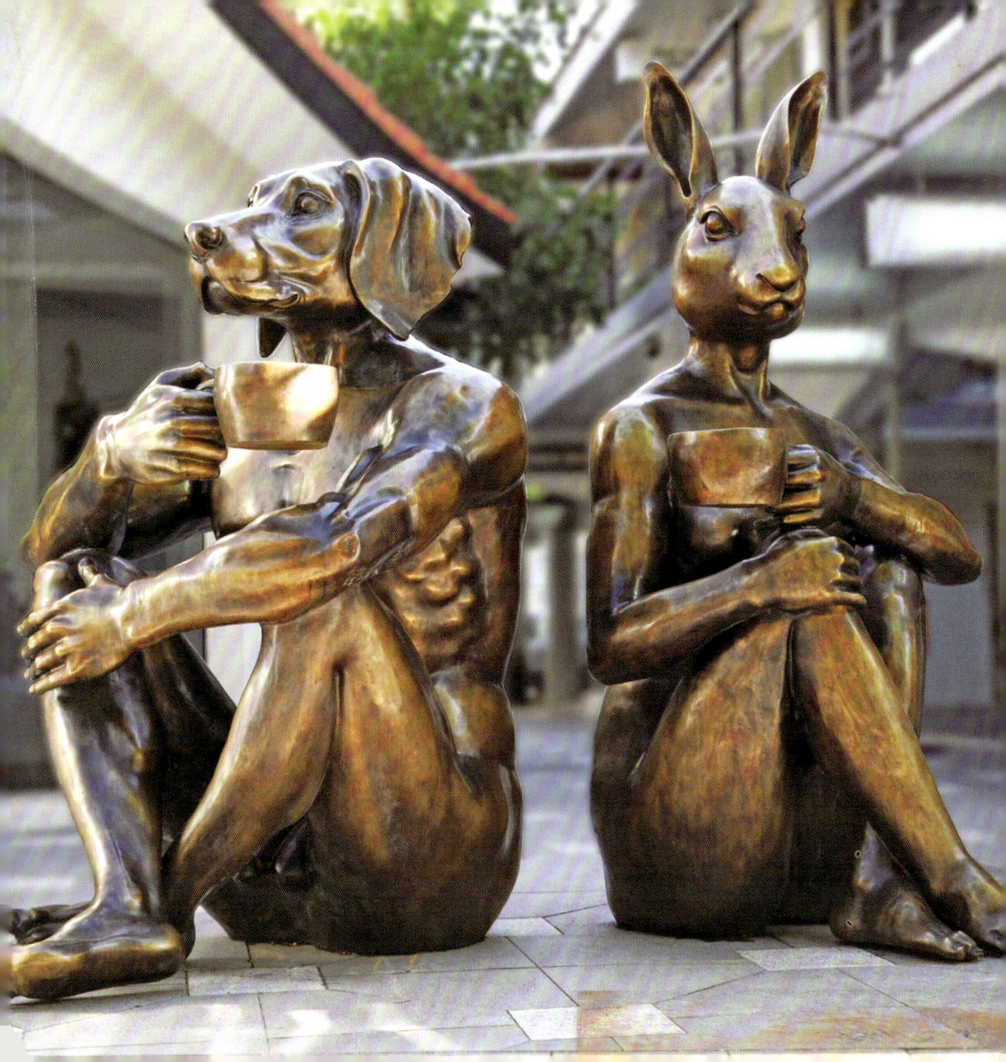

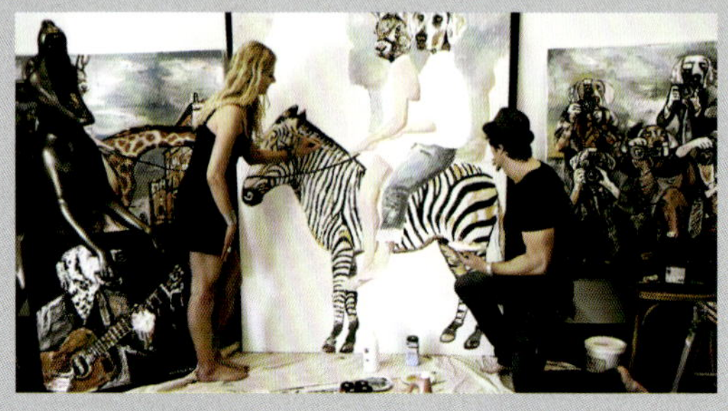

Wife and husband Gillie and Marc met in Hong Kong and began working as a creative team in the mid-1990s. The couple, both of whom had esteemed advertising backgrounds, initially painted side-by-side but soon moved to painting on one canvas, before sculpting together on one large-scale work.

Today Gillie and Marc's artworks are on public display across Australia, New Zealand, and many parts of Asia. Art lovers all over the world have also installed Gillie and Marc originals in their homes and corporate spaces. Gillie and Marc's solo exhibitions have been held in Sydney, New York, Singapore, Hong Kong and Belgium, and they have been involved in group exhibitions around the world. The pair has also won numerous awards over the years, and was a finalist in the 2006 Archibald Portrait Prize.

Joint collaboration is at the heart of everything Gillie and Marc do, whether it be painting or sculpting, illustrating or publishing books, or living life to its fullest with their two children, Jessie and Ben, and their Weimaraner Indie.